THE GRAMMATICAL STRUCTURES
OF ENGLISH AND ITALIAN

CONTRASTIVE STRUCTURE SERIES

Charles A. Ferguson

General Editor

THE GRAMMATICAL STRUCTURES OF

ENGLISH AND ITALIAN

Frederick B. Agard

and

Robert J. Di Pietro

THE UNIVERSITY OF CHICAGO PRESS
CHICAGO AND LONDON

This work was developed pursuant to a contract between
the United States Office of Education and the Center for Applied Linguistics
of the Modern Language Association, and is published with permission
of the United States Office of Education.

PC1099
A7

Library of Congress Catalog Card Number: 65-25119

The University of Chicago Press, Chicago 60637

The University of Chicago Press, Ltd., London W.C.1

© 1965 by the University of Chicago. All rights reserved. Published 1965

Second Impression 1969. Printed in the United States of America

GENERAL INTRODUCTION TO THE SERIES

This study is part of a series of contrastive structure studies which describe the similarities and differences between English and each of the five foreign languages most commonly taught in the United States: French, German, Italian, Russian, and Spanish. Each of the five languages is represented by two volumes in the series, one on the sound systems and the other on the grammatical systems of English and the language in question. The volumes on sounds make some claim to completeness within the limits appropriate to these studies; the volumes on grammar, however, treat only selected topics, since complete coverage would be beyond the scope of the series. The studies are intended to make available for the language teacher, textbook writer, or other interested reader a body of information which descriptive linguists have derived from their contrastive analyses of English and the other languages.

The Center for Applied Linguistics, in undertaking this series of studies, has acted on the conviction held by many linguists and specialists in language teaching that one of the major problems in the learning of a second language is the interference caused by the structural differences between the native language of the learner and the second language. A natural consequence of this conviction is the belief that a careful contrastive analysis of the two languages offers an excellent basis for the preparation of instructional materials, the planning of courses, and the development of actual classroom techniques.

The project got under way in the summer of 1959. The primary responsibility for the various parts of the project fell to specialists of demonstrated competence in linguistics having a strong interest in the application of linguistics to practical problems of language teaching. Wherever possible, a recognized senior scholar specializing in the foreign language was selected either as a consultant or as an author.

Since it did not seem likely that the users of the series would generally read all five studies, considerable duplication was permitted in the material presented. Also,

v

although a general framework was suggested for the studies and some attempt was made to achieve a uniformity of procedure by consultation among those working on the project, each team was given free rein to follow its own approach. As a result, the parts of the series vary in style, terminology, notation, and in the relative emphasis given to different aspects of the analysis.

Some differences in these studies are also due to the wide range of variation in American English, especially in the pronunciation of vowels. No special consideration was given to English spoken outside America since the studies were primarily intended for language teachers and textbook writers in this country. There are also differences in the studies which depend on the structure of each of the foreign languages under comparison. Thus, if a fact of English agrees well with a feature of Italian it may merit little mention, if any, in an English-Italian contrastive study, but if the same fact differs in a complicated and highly significant way from a corresponding feature of Spanish, it may require elaborate treatment in an English-Spanish study.

In the course of the project several by-products were produced, two of which are worth noting as of possible interest to readers of volumes in this series. One, Linguistic Reading Lists for Teachers of Modern Languages (Washington, D. C., 1962) was compiled chiefly by linguists working on the project and contains a carefully selected and annotated list of works which linguists would recommend to the teacher of French, German, Italian, Russian, or Spanish. The other, W. W. Gage's Contrastive Studies in Linguistics (Washington, D. C., 1961), consists of an unannotated listing of all contrastive studies which had come to the attention of the Center by the summer of 1961.

Although the value of contrastive analysis has been recognized for some time, relatively few substantial studies have been published. In a sense then this series represents a pioneering venture in the field of applied linguistics and, as with all such ventures, some of the material may eventually turn out to be of little value and some of the methods used may turn out to be inadequate. The authors and editor are fully convinced of the value of the studies, however, and hope that the series will represent an important step in the application of linguistic procedures to language problems. They are also agreed in their expectation that, while in another ten years this series may seem primitive and unsatisfactory, the principles of contrastive analysis will be more widely recognized and appreciated.

Charles A. Ferguson
Director, Center for Applied Linguistics

TABLE OF CONTENTS

THE SECOND LEVEL OF COMPARISON: GRAMMAR

1

1.0.

The companion volume to this one is a comparison of the sound systems of Italian and English. The present chapter begins the second level of comparison—that of the grammatical systems of the two languages. For reasons we are about to indicate, the treatment of grammatical differences demands some changes in our approach.

Because of the relatively few elements to be considered, it has been possible to cover the phonological systems within a comparatively short discussion; this has allowed us ample space for a point-by-point comparison between the two languages. Grammar, on the other hand, involves systems of far greater complexity. Consequently, a complete statement of the grammatical structure of each language, plus a point-by-point comparison (on the model of the phonology), would result in so detailed and rambling a disquisition as to obscure the significant contrasts.

Many readers of this section of our analysis will doubtless encounter technical terms that are new to them, and will find themselves called upon to accept reinterpretations of a few traditional concepts. In order to forestall possible confusions, it will be well to keep in mind this guiding principle: the points of reference for the definition of each term, new or traditional, are to be found within the structure of one or the other of the languages itself, rather than in the notion of a general grammar equally applicable to any and all languages. For example, the term "substantive" subsumes a class of words in Italian which corresponds to no single class in English. To put it in another way, the frames of reference used to establish parts of speech and to identify constructions in Italian are not the same frames as those used for English. Let us take the following examples from the two languages. In Italian, we will find that the word _svenimento_ is a substantive and that the word _svenire_ is a verb. All Italian substantives may be preceded by an article (definite or indefinite); most of them may also be given plural inflection. The verb is clearly marked as such by its inflection for tense-mood, person-number, and the rest. A different situation prevails in English. Take the word faint. Although it has substantival function in she fell into a faint, its function is verbal in men seldom faint and adjectival in a very faint trace of sulphur. Here the basic form of the word remains unchanged; only the functions differ. This is a feature of English grammar little shared by Italian. The grammar of every language must therefore be described strictly in terms of its own forms and functions before a valid comparison with another language can be made.

1.1. THE METHOD

The implications of the principle stated above would seem to demand a three-stage development: first, the grammar of Italian; second, the grammar of English; third, a comparison of the two. For our purposes, however, a single treatment seems less cumbersome and therefore more practical. This once-through treatment is organized on the basis of Italian, the target language, with interruptions at appropriate points for statements about English and for relevant comparisons.

One of the major tools at the disposal of the linguist for discovering grammatical structures is the "testing frame." Testing frames are simply grammatical environments which serve to bring into focus the variations in function to which a given word or phrase is subject. In the examples of faint given above, the testing frames are obviously she fell into a _____ , men seldom _____ , and a very _____ trace of sulphur. The three frames reveal three separate functions of central importance for differentiating the English parts of speech called noun, verb, and adjective. Faint is of a class that functions as all three. Such a word as trap does not, for although she fell into a trap is grammatical and shows trap to be a noun, *a very trap trace of sulphur is not grammatical and shows that trap is not an adjective. A more extensive application of the testing-frame procedure to English discloses at least seven distinct subclasses of words: those which occur as nouns only (food, action, friend, art); as adjectives only (false, likely, certain, icy); as verbs only (describe, admit, punish, apply); as nouns and verbs (walk, cure, air, change); as adjectives and verbs (clean, dry, thin, slow); as nouns and adjectives (sweet, savage, private, male); as nouns, adjectives and verbs (faint, black, sound, light). A native speaker of English can supply the requisite testing frames for any word or phrase in his lexicon.

1.2. PARTS OF SPEECH AND THE GRAMMATICAL SYSTEM

In the foregoing discussion two fundamental features of grammatical design have been mentioned: FORM and FUNCTION. As we have already suggested, the words of a language can be classified according to shared patterns of change in form and shared functional behavior. Most substantives in Italian, and most nouns in English are inflected for singular versus plural number as shown in changes of form. The seven classes of English words given above reflect seven different patterns of function. Assuming that we are clear as to the meaning of "word" (see ¶1.6 for the definition), we may define the parts of speech of a language as classes of WORDS which share similarities in form change or in function or in both. The definition must be couched in these terms, because the amount of variation in form and function is not constant for all languages or even within the grammatical framework of the same language. Latin has more variation in form than Italian. Italian has more than English. English has more than Chinese. Within both Italian and English, there are large numbers of words which show no variation in form but clearly belong to different parts of speech because they differ greatly in function. Italian contro, ecco, si, come show no variability of form, but have complete difference of function; this fact alone is sufficient to place them in different classes.

Selection of the testing frames for parts of speech necessarily involves control of another basic feature of the grammatical system: its syntactical constructions. Viewing the testing frames from a slightly different perspective, we may consider them as grammatical constructions of one or another type. Thus into a faint is a construction of the prepositional type. English and Italian share many of the same types of constructions, but they do not always use the same ones to express the same content. Instances in which Italian constructions are not matched by English ones, or in which shared constructions do not have the same privileges of occurrence, form the substance of Chapter 3.

A third feature of central importance in the description and comparison of grammatical systems is the number and types of grammatical distinctions made by each. Both Italian and English, for example, make a distinction of number: Italian casa case, English house houses. Italian also makes a grammatical distinction of gender which is lacking in English: masculine buono, feminine buona. Number, gender, tense, and the like are called grammatical categories. Each grammatical category will be discussed in connection with the part of speech it affects.

1.3. MEANING AND GRAMMATICAL ANALYSIS

Traditional grammars often employ lexical meaning to distinguish grammatical units. English and and or, for example, have been placed in different subclasses on the basis of their semantic difference: and is said to be an "additive" conjunction, whereas or is classed as an "alternative" one. A statement of this sort tends to obscure the more important fact that both and and or have essentially the same distribution and that the difference between, say, men and women and men or women is lexical rather than grammatical. It bears repeating here that one of the major contributions of linguistics to grammatical analysis is its insistence on structural criteria for the definition of grammatical units.

1.4. SYNCTACTICAL LINKAGE

Individual units in a construction are often linked together by some type of marker (I want to go; neither this nor that), or by like inflection (belle ragazze, in which both forms are feminine plural), or by some sort of cross-reference or agreement:

Questo libro non è mio;   Giovanni canta;   Maria e Giuseppe ascoltano

When there is no overt manifestation of it, the linkage is said to be by selection: black cat, big houses. Other types of linkage exist—for example, by government (Latin ex libris, ad exemplum, with the prepositions governing the case of the nouns), but the types referred to above sufficiently cover Italian and English.

1.5. THE MORPHEME

Our discussion thus far has been centered in words and their grammatical behavior. A precise linguistic definition of the word as a unit of grammar, however, must await the introduction of a more fundamental unit called the MORPHEME. Linguistics defines the morpheme as the smallest individually meaningful unit of grammar. For example, the English form cats contains two morphemes: cat (the animal) and -s (the suffix signaling plurality). Of course there is a great difference between the kinds of meaning conveyed by cat and -s, but the fact remains that both mean something. The difference is that the meaning of -s is statable only in terms of its grammatical function, whereas the meaning of cat can be given with reference to something which human experience considers to have objective existence. An investigation of all the morphemes of a language reveals that those with meanings statable only in terms of grammatical function are limited in number: English ly-, -ed, -ing, to (in to live), and so on. Those morphemes whose meanings are, like that of cat, non-grammatical (i.e., lexical) make up most of the stock: English house, man, charity, blue, angry, write, add, soon, and so on.

1.6. THE WORD AND ITS MORPHOLOGY

Words may be viewed as those units which stand midway between morphemes and syntactic constructions. The layman conceives of a word as a string of letters set off by spaces at either end. The linguist defines a word as a morphological unit—that is, either a single morpheme or a construction of morphemes made up of a STEM and one or more AFFIXES. Affixes subsume PREFIXES, INFIXES, and SUFFIXES; any of these may be either of two types: INFLECTIONAL or DERIVATIONAL. In both Italian and English, the affixes are limited to prefixes and suffixes, and prefixes are derivational only. Derivational affixes are morphemes whose meaning is referable to experience: English dis- in disappear or Italian s- in sparire; English -er in player or Italian -tore in giocatore. Inflectional suffixes are morphemes which signal the contrasts within such grammatical categories as number, gender, or tense: English -s in cats, Italian -i in gatti.

A STEM is a part—one or more morphemes—to which an inflectional or derivational affix may be added: English figure- in figured (with inflectional affix), in disfigure (with derivational affix), and in disfigured (with both); Italian vede- in vedevo (with inflectional affix), in rivede (with derivational affix), and in rivedevo (with both).

A ROOT is a single morpheme either accompanied by a derivational affix or compounded with other roots. Unlike stems, roots never occur with inflectional affixes only. An example of a root in English is -ceive-, as in conceive, perceive, receive, Italian termografo and grafologia contain the compounded roots term-, graf-, and -log-.

In English, many stems can themselves be words—for example, cat, sleep (one morpheme each, but cf. catty, cats, sleepless, sleeping). In Italian, there are fewer stems that are themselves words, because many of the substantives and all the verbs—which constitute the bulk of the lexicon—always carry inflectional suffixes. But in both English and Italian, many words consist of a single morpheme which is neither a stem nor a root: English then, Italian allora.

1.7. DERIVATION

DERIVATION is the process of stem formation whereby much of the lexicon of a language is constructed. In this process there are two types of stem: SIMPLE STEMS, consisting of one morpheme only (Italian ragazz- or governa-, English fast- or govern-); DERIVATIVES, which consist of more than one morpheme. The latter type is subdivided into secondary derivatives, with at least one of its components a stem (Italian ri-pensa, English dis-cover-), and primary derivatives, with none of its components a stem (Italian col-loca-, grafo-log-ia, English grapho-log-y).

Actually, the student need not know the difference between a stem and a root. He should, however, be aware of which affixes are inflectional and which are derivational. And he should be made to understand that derivational affixation, as well as inflectional, is much more active in Italian than in English; we do not find English derivational affixes as widely used as, say, Italian -in-, -ett-, or -one- (as in ragazzino, ragazzetto, ragazzone). A thorough understanding of the processes of derivation in Italian is of the greatest value to the teacher who wishes to construct effective vocabulary drills.

1.8. MORPHOPHONEMICS

In any language, a given morpheme may occur in more than one actual phonemic shape. Thus, for example, the English inflectional affixes /-z, -əz, -s/ in dogs, horses, cats constitute three variant phonemic shapes of a single morpheme meaning "plural number." Alternant shapes or morphs that group together as members of a single morpheme are said to be allomorphs of that morpheme, just as some variant sounds or phones are classed together as allophones of a given phoneme. And just as allophones are conditioned by their surrounding sounds, so allomorphs are determined by their environment and thus stand in complementary distribution, not in contrast. Allomorphs are conditioned either phonologically or morphologically. A classic example of phonologic conditioning is that of the English plural allomorphs cited above. The basic allomorph is /-z/ as in dogs, eyes, ears, but phonologically /z/ may not occur after a voiceless consonant, and therefore automatically becomes the voiceless /-s/ in tops, decks, cats; neither /z/ nor /s/ may occur after /s z š ž č ǧ/, and therefore a vowel is introduced to yield /-əz/ in horses, sizes, dishes, matches. On the other hand, English irregular plurals such as oxen, children, feet, mice are good examples of morphological conditioning: these stems could, phonologically, have a regular plural allomorph—compare, the possessive forms ox's, child's, foot's, mouse's—but they unpredictably require a different one. Often it is possible to predict morphologically conditioned allomorphs within a given subsystem such as that of regular verbs or the like. For example, in Italian, the verb suffixes -ino in cantino and -ano in vendano are allomorphs of the present subjunctive third plural morpheme and are seen to be in complementary distribution once we know the "conjugations"— that is, the stem classes. Thus we can predict that the allomorph in question will be -ino for any regular verb having -a- before the infinitive suffix -re (so mangiare : mangino) and will be -ano for any regular verb having -e- or -i- in that position (so temere : temano or partire : partano).

Some morphemes have allomorphs in "free" alternation; that is, there is no conditioning factor, and the speaker is free to select one or the other without a contrast in meaning, as, for example, either -rono or -ttero as the preterit third plural suffix of a verb like credere : crederono or credettero, or either dev- or debb- as the stem allomorph before the present first singular suffix -o in dovere.

The descriptive analysis of morphemes—that is, the alternating phonemic shapes of allomorphs in accordance with their phonologic or morphologic environment— is called rather forbiddingly MORPHOPHONEMICS. The morphophonemics of Italian inflection, in both stems and suffixes, is considerably more complex than that of English, especially in the verb system; this constitutes a major factor of difference between the two languages. It will accordingly be given full coverage in the next chapter, under each part of speech in turn.

GRAMMATICAL FORMS: [2]
THE PARTS OF SPEECH

2.0.

      This chapter is concerned primarily with the word as a unit of grammar. We establish the parts of speech of Italian and describe their morphology. Relevant comparisons with English parts of speech are included as an integral part of each section.

      As we pointed out in ¶1.2, identification of parts of speech involves some inevitable reference to syntax, through the use of testing frames. In the discussion it will therefore be necessary to make occasional cross-references to material treated in Chapter 3. We are aware that such a procedure tends to make for slow reading, and we can only ask the reader's indulgence. The cross-reference method represents an effort to achieve a middle ground: that of piecemeal presentation without losing sight of the structure as a whole.

2.1. VERBS

      The verbs of Italian are those words which may have complements of various types—for example, an accusative complement as in <u>vedo il cane</u>, or an attributive complement as in <u>stanno qui</u>. The small set of verbally bound PRO-COMPLEMENTS (established as a class in ¶2.2) furnish the most convenient frame for establishing the verb as a part of speech. That is to say, any word occurring in construction with a pro-complement, either before it or after it, is by definition a verb: <u>mi alzo</u>, <u>ti credo</u>, <u>si dice</u>, <u>uscirne</u>, <u>avendolo</u>, <u>eccole</u>. Verbs are one of the two largest word classes of the language; the other is substantives (¶2.3).

      Needless to say, English also has verbs. The best frame for establishing them as a class is probably Personal Pronoun Subject + _____; thus, for example, <u>I see</u>, <u>we know</u>, <u>you can</u>, show the words <u>see</u>, <u>know</u>, <u>can</u> to be verbs.

The morphological behavior of the Italian verb is extremely complex—infinitely more so than that of the English verb. It is therefore in the attempt to master this part of speech that the English-speaking student of Italian finds his greatest concentration of genuine problems and onerous difficulties: problems in coping with the numerous morphemic distinctions made by inflection—most of which it is true have counterparts in English verb phrase structure; yet the transfer of syntactic habits to the domain of inflection is always a wrench—and difficulties in merely learning the unpredictable vagaries of the morphophonemic alternations.

Both Italian and English verbs are inflected for various grammatical categories, and in both there are two major inflectional subclasses set apart by both morphological and syntactic behavior: the FINITE and the NON-FINITE. In Italian, the dichotomy is complete. The finite forms of a verb are those which inflect for tense, mood, person, and number; which are preceded by accompanying pro-complements, and which enjoy none of the syntactic privileges of the non-finites. The non-finite forms, on the other hand, are those which do not inflect for tense, mood, person, and number, which are followed by accompanying pro-complements, which combine syntactically with auxiliaries and modals in verb phrases, and so on, as we shall see. The typical Italian verb has thirty-nine finite forms and eight non-finite forms, with practically no overlap in shapes.

In English, the finite/non-finite cleavage is based on the same general sorts of morphological and syntactical distinction, but there is overlapping of forms. One basic or general form of the verb fills both finite and non-finite slots; two forms are exclusively finite; and two are always non-finite, for a total of five as against the forty-seven of Italian.

2.1.1. THE FINITES

It is defensible to say, and it has been said traditionally, that the Italian finite verb is inflected to contrast five tenses, two moods, three persons, and two numbers. Descriptive analysis would, however, require that if this were true, we should be able to isolate inflectional morphemes for each of the four categories. But this does not prove to be true, since there is no way to determine, on the one hand, what part of the inflectional ending of, say, cantasse signals past tense and what part signals subjunctive mood; or, on the other hand, what part of the ending of canterò means first person and what part means singular. Furthermore, it is clear that some tenses, such as the future or conditional, do not inflect for mood at all. And is cantasse the subjunctive counterpart of cantava or of cantò? We shall be on sounder analytical ground if we hold that the Italian finite verb inflects in just two ways: for tense/mood (T/M) and for person/number (P/N).

We can then go on to state that there are seven T/M morphemes, which signal respectively present, present subjunctive, imperfect, preterit, past subjunctive, future, and conditional; and that there are six P/N morphemes which signal respectively first singular, second singular, third singular, first plural, second plural, and third plural. In some forms, it is possible to correlate the two inflectional morphemes with discrete phonemic shapes; for example, in <u>cantavamo</u>, it is clear enough that <u>-va-</u> is the allomorph of the imperfect, and <u>-mo</u> the allomorph of the first plural. On the other hand, no cut of the ending of <u>canterebbe</u> would be satisfactory; nor can we cut at all the <u>-o</u> of <u>canto</u>, which nonetheless contains two morphemes: present, and first singular.

2.1.1.1. REGULAR FINITES

The separation of stems from endings is a simple enough matter. Rapid inspection of such partial sets as:

cantate	cantavate	cantaste	canterete
vendete	vendevate	vendeste	venderete
sentite	sentivate	sentiste	sentirete

allows us to isolate the stems <u>canta-</u> (with the one alternant <u>cante-</u>), <u>vende-</u>, <u>senti-</u>. Since all stems turn out to end in one of these three vowels, it is convenient to speak of <u>a</u>-stems, <u>e</u>-stems, and <u>i</u>-stems. Since <u>e</u>-stems and <u>i</u>-stems share some features as against <u>a</u>-stems, it is often convenient to subsume the two as <u>e/i</u>-stems.

The following tabulation shows the forty-one endings which recur with every regular finite.

		Present	Pres. Subj.	Impf.	Pret.	Past Subj.	Future	Cond.
1 s.		-o		-vo	-i	-ssi	-ró	-réi
2 s.		-i	-i/-a	-vi	-sti	-ssi	-rái	-résti
3	s.	-a/-e		-va	——	-sse	-rá	-rébbe
	p.	-ano/-ono	-ino/-ano	-vano	-rono	-ssero	-ránno	-rébbero
1	p.	→	-iámo	-vámo	-mmo	-ssimo	-rémo	-rémmo
2		-te	-iáte	-váte	-ste	-ste	-réte	-réste

Phonemic stresses, where present, are marked in order to facilitate observation of stress patterning, which is wholly systematic. Indeed, there is much more system than meets the eye in Italian inflection as a whole, and much more than the English-speaking student can be expected to discover for himself, unaccustomed as he is to multiple inflection no matter how neatly patterned. With a minimum of further statements, we shall have accounted for all features of the pattern.

The seven T/M's fall into three subgroups, which we may designate for convenience as present, past, and future respectively. Each subgroup has distinctive characteristics, as follows.

In the present set, stress is inherent in the center of the stem—that is, in some syllable preceding the final vowel of the stem. This STEM VOWEL itself is canceled by any vowel-initial ending, so that canta- plus -o yields cánt-o, vende- plus -ano yields vénd-ano, and so on. If there is more than one syllable before the stem vowel, the location of the center is not predictable and must be learned for each verb—for example, command-a, cápit-a.

Some of the endings vary according to the stem class, as separated by the diagonal lines in the table. To the left of the lines are the a-stem endings, to the right the e/i-stem endings. There are two areas of ambiguity. The allomorphs -i/-a of the present subjunctive mark only singular, making no distinction as to first, second, or third person; in the a-stems, -i further fails to distinguish present subjunctive singular from present second singular. The ending -iámo does not differentiate present from present subjunctive. This ending occupies the present subjunctive slot in the table because of its clear congruity with the present subjunctive second plural -iáte; this is the meaning of the arrow in the present slot.

Whenever -mo or -te is present as the final shape, the stress is displaced to the vowel immediately before it—either the stem vowel itself, as in cantá-te, vendé-te, or the -a- of the ending, as in cant-iámo, vend-iáte.

In the past set, stress is inherent in the stem vowel. When -mo or -te is present, this stress is displaced to the preceding -a- of the imperfect ending—for example, canta-vámo, canta-váte, as against cantá-vo, cantá-i, cantá-ssi (even cantá-ssimo), and so on.

The preterit third singular is entered on the table as a blank, or "zero," ending, because of the e/i-stem forms vendé, sentí which seem to consist of bare stem. It is therefore logical to take the a-stem form cantó likewise as bare stem plus zero ending, with the stem vowel alternating to -ó in this one position (it is interesting to note that a regular form cantá does exist in some dialects, though not in the standard language).

In the future T/M's, stress is inherent in the vowel immediately following the characteristic -r-, and never varies. Historically these T/M's are derived from the infinitive form (with ending -re) plus an inflected auxiliary, but descriptively there is no valid reason to analyze them this way for present-day Italian. In the instance of a-stems, the shape cante- and so on which precedes the endings may be taken merely as the stem with an alternant stem vowel before the -r-.

Further analysis might attempt to break the endings displayed in the table down into two morphs each: one of T/M, and one of P/N. This is easy to do in part. The final shape -mo appears in every first plural form, -te in every second plural form, and either -no or -ro in every third plural form. Equally isolable are the T/M markers -va-, imperfect, and -sse-, past subjunctive. When, however, it comes to breaking the preterit or the future or the conditional into separate T/M and P/N components, such manipulations and provisos would be required as to render the whole procedure very questionable. It would certainly be unnecessarily complex for the average English-speaking student of Italian, who in any event is not prepared for such inflectional possibilities as the separate and successive marking of T/M and P/N, given his comparatively simple verb morphology, in which no finite verb form ever marks more than one category at a time.

Let us here turn to the English system.

In the finite set, there is only a vestige of inflection for mood, and there is just one suffix of tense—the past morpheme, which in all regular verbs has three phonologically predictable allomorphs added to the basic form:

/t/ after final /p t č k f Θ s/: like liked (/láyk láykt/)
/əd/ after final /t d/: mend mended (/ménd méndəd/)
/d/ elsewhere: die died (/dáy dáyd/).

When the past morpheme is present, there is no inflection for P/N. The present tense is signaled merely by absence of past inflection (for this reason, among others, some analysts prefer to call it the "non-past"). If the subject of a non-past finite is third singular, a morpheme marking this fact is added to the basic form:

/s/ after final /p t k f Θ/: like likes (/láyk láyks/)
/əz/ after final /s z š ž č ǧ/: catch catches (/kǽč kǽčəz/)
/z/ elsewhere: cry cries (/kráy kráyz/)

This distribution of allomorphs is identical to those of the plural morpheme and of the possessive morpheme for nouns. When the subject is other than third singular, only the syntactic environment marks the verb—in its base form—as finite. A vestigial distinction of mood is made by many (though by no means all) speakers of English and in formal written English: the omission of the third singular suffix with third singular subjects as a signal of "subjunctive"—for example, we insist that he go.

The unique verb <u>be</u> allows for two elsewhere nonexistent distinctions, through irregular morphological variation: in the non-past, a first singular form <u>am</u> and a generalized plural form <u>are</u>, both in contrast with the basic form <u>be</u> and the third singular form <u>is</u>; in the irregularly formed past, a singular/plural contrast <u>was</u> : <u>were</u> (<u>you</u> being taken as always plural grammatically).

Since a finite is obligatorily accompanied by a subject in English, the third singular morpheme is non-functional and automatic (except in the recessive <u>he goes</u> : <u>he go</u> contrast). This being so, the English speaker is not in a good position to understand the morphemic value of Italian P/N inflection when finites occur without a syntactically separate subject, as they so often do. Compare these minimal utterances in the two languages:

P/N distinction provided by contrasting inflection alone			P/N distinction provided by subjects: third singular -s non-functional
	Lavor<u>o</u>.	I work.	
	Lavor<u>iamo</u>.	We work.	
	Lavor<u>a</u>.	He work<u>s</u>.	

2.1.1.2. IRREGULAR FINITES

Irregularities in verb morphology are a characteristic feature of many languages, including Italian and English. In the English finites, the irregularities are mostly of one type: the past tense is formed by a change in the shape of the stem, to which the addition or not of the regular past ending is then largely irrelevant: <u>run ran</u>, <u>bring brought</u>, <u>keep kept</u> (cf. <u>kep</u> in many dialects). The irregularities in the non-past, besides <u>be</u>, are: <u>have has</u> (/hǽv hǽz/), <u>do does</u> (/dúw dǝ́z/), and <u>say says</u> (/séy séz/). In Italian finites also, irregularities are confined mainly to non-functional variations of stems; except to an extent in the preterit, the endings remain constant. Stem alternations may be classified to some extent, as follows.

2.1.1.3. PREDICTABLE ALTERNATIONS

Among the <u>a</u>-stems, a number have an <u>-i-</u> (never stressed) immediately before the stem vowel—for example, <u>stúdia-</u>, <u>inízia-</u>. Any <u>i</u>-initial ending of the present T/M's not only cancels the stem vowel as usual but also fuses with the preceding <u>-i-</u> into a single phoneme, so that, for example, <u>studia-</u> plus <u>-i</u> yields <u>studi</u>; <u>studia-</u> plus <u>-iamo</u> yields <u>studiamo</u>, <u>inizia-</u> plus <u>-iate</u> yields <u>iniziate</u>.

Among the <u>e/i</u>-stems, a number have the phonemes /č̆/, /ğ̆/, or /š̆š̆/ before the stem vowel: <u>vince-</u>, <u>legge-</u>, <u>nasce-</u>. These palatal consonants alternate to the non-palatal phonemes /k/, /g/, and /sk/ respectively whenever the ending-initial vowel <u>-o-</u>

or -a- cancels the stem vowel. (When the consonant is double, both of course alternate together.) So we get vinco(no) vinca(no) as against vinci vincete, leggo(no) legga(no) as against legge leggiamo, nasco(no) nasca(no) as against nasce nasciamo. We observe that the initial -i- of the endings -iamo -iate is absorbed by these palatal consonants: vinciamo = /vinčámo/, leggiamo = /leǧǧámo/, nasciamo = /naššámo/. The same is true in a-stems which have a (non-alternating) palatal: baciamo = /bačámo/, mangiate = /manǧáte/, lasciate = /laššáte/; and in all stems with palatal /ɲɲ/ or /ʎʎ/: bagniamo = /baɲɲámo/, sbagliamo = /sbaʎʎámo/, scegliate = /šeʎʎáte/.

In the subclass of centerless a-stems are two stems which have no center, and so consist merely of consonant plus inherently stressed stem vowel: dá- and stá-. These have some automatic features in the present T/M's, where the unstressed vowel-initial endings are added to the stem vowel. Thus dá- plus -o yields dó (with cancellation but retention of the stress of the ending); dá- plus -i yields dái (without cancellation, cf. the preterit first singular); dá- plus -a yields dá (with fusion); dá- plus -ano yields dánno (with fusion and doubling of the -n-). In the present subjunctive, the stem vowel shifts to -i- whereas the endings become those of an e/i-stem, yielding día(no) and, with fusion of -i-'s, diámo diáte. In the future T/M's the stem vowel remains -a- rather than alternating to -e- — for example, daró, darei. Centerless a-stems appear here and there as unpredictable alternants among the highly irregular verbs; where they occur the pattern is always the same: in anda- the short stem vá- yields va vai vanno, in face- the short fá-yields fa fai fanno fate and the future stem far-, in sape- the short sá- yields so sa sai sanno, and in esse- the short sá- yields the present subjunctive sía(no) siamo siate and the future stem sar-.

In any not otherwise irregular e/i-stem having one of the lone consonants /n l/or one of their (doubled) palatal correlates /ɲɲ ʎʎ/ before the stem vowel, a -g- is added before the endings -o(no) and -a(no): rimane-: rimango(no) rimanga(no) as against rimane rimaniamo; sali-: salgo(no) salga(no) as against sale salíte. The double palatals /ɲɲ ʎʎ/become /n l/ respectively before the added -g-: spegne-(e):[1] spengo(no) spenga-(no) as against spegne spegnete; scioglie-(ɔ): sciolgo(no) sciolga(no) as against scioglie sciogliamo.

In e/i-stems having the lone consonant /r/ before the stem vowel, this -r-is replaced by the vowel -i- before the endings -o(no) -a(no): pare-: paio(no) paia(no) as against pare pariamo etc.

---

1. For explanation of these parenthesized symbols, see the following section.

2.1.1.4. UNPREDICTABLE ALTERNATIONS

Present Stems.— Wherever the stress, by reason of stem-vowel cancellation, recedes to an -e- or an -o- as the center of the stem, the resulting stressed vowel phoneme is unpredictable as between /e/ and /ɛ/ on the one hand, or /o/ and /ɔ/ on the other hand. So, for example, the result is /e/ in vende-: vénd-, but /ɛ/ in legge-: lègg-; /o/ in soffri-: sòffr- but /ɔ/ in copri-: còpr-. As the second member of a dipthonged center, the stressed vowel is always /ɛ/ in -ie- and /ɔ/ in -uo-—for example, vieta-: vièt-; suona-: suòn-. Otherwise, however, the vowel needs to be marked in a notation of the stem: leva- (ɛ), crede- (e), tórna- (ɔ). In a handful of e/i- stems, the stressed occurrences of center -e- and -o- turn up as the respective diphthongs /iɛ/ and /uɔ/—for example, sede-: sièd-; move-: muòv-. These instances can be flagged in the same manner: sede- (iɛ), move- (uɔ). Note that the addition of -g- inhibits any diphthonging of a center -e- or -o- that may occur in the g-less forms; thus veni- (iɛ): vieni viene but vengo(no) venga(no); dole- (uɔ): duoli duole but dolgo(no) dolga(no).

Among the i-stems, more verbs than not are augmented by the addition of the cluster -sc-—in two phonemic shapes: /ʃ̆ʃ̆/ before -i -e, /sk/ before -o(no) -a(no)—before the unstressed vowel initial inflections. As a result no cancellation occurs, and the stem vowel retains the stress throughout; thus, capisco(no), capisca(no), capisci, capisce, as well as capite, capiamo, capiate. Membership of an i-stem in this subclass is not in itself predictable and the stem should be marked to indicate it: capi(sc)-, puli(sc)-, as compared with unaugmented parti-, dormi- (ɔ).

A number of common verbs, most of them e/i-stems, have an alternant stem in the first singular, third singular, and third plural forms of the preterit. This stem is characterized by a final unstressed -e, with the stress inherent in the center (hence the designation "strong" preterit). The endings are the regular ones, except that the third plural -rono is reduced to -ro because of the stress pattern. For example, in the verb prende- (ɛ), which has the strong preterit stem prése-, the forms affected are the first singular presi (the ending -i cancels the stem vowel as expected), the third singular prese, and the third plural presero. The remaining three preterit forms of such a verb do not have the strong stem alternant and are therefore wholly regular: prendesti, prendemmo, prendeste.

In several e/i-stems, the stem vowel is dropped out before the initial -r- of all the future T/M endings. The result is a cluster: ave-: av-r-; vede- (e): ved-r-. These stems are called "syncopated." The privilege of the stem vowel of clustering with /r/ does not, however, automatically cause the syncopation: it does not occur, for example, in crede- (e): crede-r-; it sometimes occurs where an impossible result is re-solved as double /rr/: rimane-: rimar-r-.

2.1.2. THE NON-FINITES

The Italian non-finite verbs are not only mutually exclusive with the finite set in syntactic environment but are also mutually exclusive with each other as to privileges of occurrence. They are a class of four: imperative, infinitive, gerund, and participle.[2] Their respective endings, as distinct from the finite endings, mark their syntactic functions as follows: imperative, singular -a/-i, plural -te; infinitive, -re; gerund, -ndo; participle, present -nte, past, -to.

2.1.2.1. REGULAR NON-FINITES

The imperative is inflected for number, with the singular marked by -a in a-stems and by -i in e/i-stems. These endings, being unstressed vowels, cancel the unstressed stem vowel and the stress strikes the center. It so happens, then, that in a-stems the imperative singular is identical in form to the finite present third singular, whereas in e/i-stems it is identical to the finite present second singular: cant-a, vend-i, sent-i. The imperative plural is identical in all regular verbs to the finite present second plural: canta-te, vende-te, senti-te.

In the infinitive, gerund, and participle, stress is inherent in the stem vowel, which never varies before the infinitive ending -re: canta-re, teme-re, apri-re. Before the gerund ending -ndo, the stem vowel of i-stems as well as of e-stems is -e- (/ɛ/): so canta-ndo, teme-ndo, and also sente-ndo. Before the participle ending -to, the stem vowel of e-stems is -u-: so canta-to, senti-to, but vendu-to.

The participle ending -to undergoes secondary inflection for G/N concord after the manner of a four-form substantive (i.e., the regular -o -i -a -e), as determined by various syntactic constructions. This secondary inflection is discussed in ¶3.1.2.2.

The English non-finite forms are two in number: the gerund and the participle.[3] The gerund is marked, for every verb in the language, by the addition of -ing to the basic form. The participle, for regular verbs, adds the allomorphs /-t -əd -d/ in the same phonologically determined distribution as the past tense and is thus identical there-

---

2. These last two are also known as the present participle and the past participle respectively, but these more traditional terms can seem misleading.

3. Morphologically, there is no imperative or infinitive. Syntactically, the imperative is the general form, and what is often called the "infinitive" is also the general form, sometimes preceded by to. See also Note 7.

with in form: <u>worked</u>, <u>mended</u>, <u>cried</u>. Some irregular verbs also have past tense and participle identical: <u>make</u>, <u>made</u>, <u>made</u>; <u>teach</u>, <u>taught</u>, <u>taught</u>; others show a distinction: <u>take</u>, <u>took</u>, <u>taken</u>; <u>sing</u>, <u>sang</u>, <u>sung</u>. The prevalent identity of past tense and participle, as well as the total absence of formal imperative and infinitive, may be expected to make of the Italian non-finite still another difficult morphological problem for the English-speaking student.

2.1.2.2. IRREGULAR NON-FINITES

All irregularities within this Italian subsystem are unpredictable. In the imperative, a small number of verbs use an alternant present stem before the imperative endings and replace <u>-te</u> with <u>-iate</u> in the plural: <u>ave- abb-i</u> <u>abb-iate</u>. If the alternant is a centerless <u>a</u>-stem, the imperative singular is like the finite third singular as in regular <u>a</u>-stems; so <u>face-</u>: imperative singular and present third singular <u>fa</u> (cf. <u>dá- dá</u>).

In a large number of <u>e</u>-stems, the stress on the infinitive recedes to the center: <u>scríve-re</u>. These are the "strong" infinitives. In <u>-e-</u> or <u>-o-</u> centers, the resulting stressed vowel phoneme is the same as in the finite present: <u>prende-</u> (e) <u>préndere</u>, <u>legge-</u> (ε) <u>lèggere</u>, <u>corre-</u> (o) <u>córrere</u>, <u>morde-</u> (ɔ) <u>mòrdere</u>, <u>coce-</u> (uɔ) <u>cuòcere</u>. In some instances, as an extra irregularity, the stem vowel is dropped and the resulting cluster resolved as /rr/: <u>pone-</u> (o) <u>pórre</u>, <u>conduce-</u> <u>condurre</u>.

A number of common <u>e/i</u>-stems have an alternant stem for the participle, with no stem vowel and therefore having strong stress placement: <u>vede-</u> (e) <u>vís-to</u>, <u>face-</u> <u>fát-to</u>. These are the "strong" participles. Many of these verbs also have strong preterits, and in a few instances the stem alternants are the same for both, with the participle ending reduced to <u>-o</u> and so canceling the stem vowel appearing in the preterit: <u>prende-</u> (e) <u>prése-</u> <u>prés-o</u>.

In the Appendix are displayed all the common irregular verbs of Italian.

2.2. THE PRO-COMPLEMENTS

Traditionally grouped with the pronouns (¶2.4), these are the monosyllabic, stressless words which occur joined phonologically to a verb, either before or after it. (For specific statements of positioning, see ¶3.1.1.1.) Their unique occurrence with, and inseparability from, a verb is sufficient to establish them as a separate part of speech. They are best called "pro-complements" because they substitute for various types of complements in verb phrases—for example, accusative complement <u>il gatto</u> in <u>lo vedo</u> (→ <u>vedo il gatto</u>); for dative complement <u>a Flavio</u> in <u>gli do il vino</u> (→ <u>do il vino a Flavio</u>). Altogether the pro-complements constitute a class of nine as follows:

Four non-third-person morphemes, mi, ti, ci_1, vi_1, correlated exclusively with the personal pronouns me, te, noi, voi. They function both as pro-accusatives (replacing me, and so on, as in mi vedono) and as pro-datives (replacing a me, and so on, as in mi dicono).

Two third-person singular non-reflexive pro-dative morphemes: gli, and le. The form gli (as in gli dico) replaces phrases of the type a lui or a + substantive-naming-a-male: a Giovanni, a quell'uomo. The form le (as in le dico) replaces a lei (including a Lei regardless of sex) or a + substantive-naming-a-female: a mia moglie, ad Annamaria. There is no third-person plural pro-dative in the set; to replace a loro or a + substantive-naming-persons, use is made of the pronoun loro itself, which of course does not form part of a verb core since it is stressed and takes the same position as a dative complement: so dico loro like dico agli amici. This gap in the system has led to a present-day situation in which many speakers of standard Italian use gli as a plural pro-dative also; for this increasing number of speakers, then, gli dico and dico loro have coalesced as gli dico.[4]

One third-person non-reflexive pro-accusative stem, l-, which is inflected like a four-form substantive (see ¶2.3.2.2) for cross-reference to the replaced accusative complement. For example, lo as in lo vedo replaces il libro or the like; la as in la vedo replaces la casa or the like; and similarly for the plural forms li and le. The singular suffixes -o, -a are optionally elided before a vowel-initial verb: lo aspetto or la aspetto → l'aspetto (but always li aspetto, le aspetto).

One third-person reflexive-reciprocal morpheme, si, correlated with the reflexive pronoun sè and functioning as both a pro-accusative and a pro-dative, replacing sè (or l'uno l'altro) as in si alzano, and a sè (or l'uno all'altro) as in si scrivono.[5]

Two pro-attributive morphemes: $ci_2 \sim vi_2$, and ne. The first replaces a space adverb such as qui or lî, or a subordinate phrase expressing space relation (alla casa, sotto l'albero) as in ci vanno or vi erano. The second, ne, replaces a subordinate phrase with di or da + axis (del denaro, da Napoli) as in ne vorrei or ne vengo. The forms ci_2 and vi_2 are never in contrast with one another; they are allomorphs in free alternation (so, ci sono or vi sono) except that in the presence of ci_1 only vi_2 occurs (ci vi rechiamo) whereas in the presence of vi_1 only ci_2 occurs (vi ci recate).

---

4. See discussion on pronouns in Robert A. Hall, Jr., Italian For Modern Living (Ithaca, N. Y.: Cornell University Press, 1959).

5. The si which often occurs in intransitive clauses (non si può, si sta bene qui) is simply not the same word as the pro-complement; see ¶3.3.1.2.

Proper use of the pro-complements constitutes a major problem for the English-speaking student of Italian, since English has no analogous part of speech—no comparable mechanism for replacing complements in verb phrases. An entirely new grammatical habit—that of replacement of some complements by adding an element to the verbal core under exacting rules of position—must be developed. Further discussion of the pro-complements relative to the verbal core is in ¶3.1.1.1.

2.3. SUBSTANTIVES

Italian substantives, the other of the two largest word classes (along with verbs), are best defined functionally as those words which occur as the center of phrases containing the definite article (¶2.5). That is, any word that will fill the blank "slot" in the testing frame [Definite Article + _____] is by definition a substantive in Italian: so pane in il pane (è cotto), donna in la donna (è mobile), difficile in il difficile (è prendere i ladri), bello in il bello (deve ancora venire), possibile in (farò tutto) il possibile, magnifico in (Lorenzo) il magnifico. As a class, substantives share other grammatical behavior, but none so inclusive as occurrence with the definite article. Most of them, for example, show number contrast: ragazzo ragazzi, femmina femmine, grande grandi. Many of them show gender contrast: amico amica, bello bella, brutto brutta. Most also may occur as attributes in substantive phrases: bianco in vino bianco, brutta in una brutta giornata, stazione in il capo stazione, lampo in la chiusura lampo.

2.3.1. THE TWO MAIN TYPES OF SUBSTANTIVE

Although Italian substantives are identified and defined by their occurrence as centers in which one of their modifiers, or attributes, is the definite article, they themselves also function widely as attributes to another substantive which is the center (see ¶3.1.2). It is only on the basis of their occurrence as attributes that substantives are divisible into two types. Type I are those which, when they occur as attributes, are not linked to the center by any gender or number agreement. Type II are those which, when attributive, always agree with the center—all of them in number, and many of them also in gender.

Most Type I substantives occur infrequently as attributes. Some noteworthy instances are spada in pesce-spada and lupo in cane-lupo, the plural forms of which are pesci-spada and cani-lupo; proper names attributive to preceding titles, as in il signor Giallo, la dottoressa Romano, il maresciallo Centofanti; attributive place names, as in Via Veneto, Piazza Cavour; month names in dates, as in il primo maggio, il venticinque dicembre. Another instance, mostly limited to written Italian but gaining in frequency, is that exemplified by capo ufficio, caduta massi, sala macchine, listino prezzi, deposito bagagli. In all such instances, the second substantive is attributive to the first. Further random examples of Type I substantives are uomo, donna, pesce, casa, treno, latte, pranzo, mano, testa, professore, azione, città, sentimento.

Type II substantives occur frequently as attributes: vecchi-[6] in un vecchio amico, una vecchia signora, vecchi libri, vecchie mura; or nemic- in l'esercito nemico, una razza nemica, soldati nemici, le truppe nemiche; or inglese-[6] in zuppa inglese, i turisti inglesi. Further random examples of Type II are nuov-, brutt-, piccol-, sporc-, giovane-, possibile-, amabile-, artista-, idiota-, ladr-, amic-, onorevole-, comunista-, lavoratore-.

In this classification, we deliberately avoid identifying Type I substantives with "nouns" and Type II substantives with "adjectives," because we hold that the distinction traditionally made on that basis is inaccurate and can be misleading to the English-speaking student. In English, to be sure, the traditional distinction between nouns and adjectives as parts of speech actually has a valid basis in the facts of the language: nouns are words which inflect for number and possession (man, men, man's, men's); adjectives inflect for neither category, but many of them inflect for comparison (new, newer, newest). But if the English speaker is allowed to take for granted that Italian also has nouns and adjectives merely "because all languages do" or for some like reason, he may attempt to differentiate them on the false basis of semantic equivalence and so assume, for example, that Italian ladr- is a noun because English thief is, or that Italian vecchi- is an adjective because English old is. We shall therefore continue to speak, for the present, only of Type I and Type II substantives in Italian. Later, in describing the substantive phrase (¶3.1.2), we shall distinguish noun and adjective functions of both types of substantive.

2.3.2. SUBSTANTIVE INFLECTION

The Italian substantive of either type has two inflectional subclasses: two-form substantives, inflected with one morpheme for plural (formula: stem ± P); and four-form substantives, inflected with four morphemes for combinations of gender and number (formula: stem + G/N).

---

6. Neither vecchio nor vecchia can logically take precedence over the other as a citation form for this substantive. It is therefore convenient to list such substantives by their stem alone, with the hyphen to indicate the potential addition of any one of four gender/number suffixes. Substantives like inglese- or facile- which may be said to have no suffix in the singular form, may nevertheless also be marked with the hyphen to indicate that they are of Type II.

2.3.2.1. TWO-FORM SUBSTANTIVES

The formula "stem ± P" indicates that the stem and the singular forms are identical and that the plural suffix may or may not be added. For example:

Stem − P: casa   (one morpheme = singular)

Stem + P : cas-e   (two morphemes = plural)[7]

The plural morpheme P has four morphologically conditioned allomorphs: -i ~ -e ~ -a ~ zero. The stem classes are as follows:

Nearly all those ending in -o (i.e., o-stems), which add -i :[8]

giorno giorni   anno anni   mano mani

A few o-stems easily listable, which add -a :

muro mura   braccio braccia   uovo uova

Almost all a-stems, which add -e :

via vie   testa teste   scarpa scarpe

A few a-stems which add -i :

duca duchi   poeta poeti   problema problemi

All e-stems, which add -i :

mese mesi   inglese inglesi   grande grandi

All stressed-vowel or consonant-final stems, plus a few oddments, which add zero and therefore have plural forms identical with the stem and singular:

città   caffè   lunedì

film   tram   lapis

auto   specie   analisi

2.3.2.2. FOUR-FORM SUBSTANTIVES

The formula stem + G/N indicates that the stem itself never occurs as a word and that one of four G/N suffixes is always added to it. These are:

Masculine-Singular (m/s)   -o   Masculine-Plural (m/p)   -i

Feminine-Singular (f/s)   -a   Feminine-Plural (f/p)   -e

Examples:

nuov-   { nuovo nuovi   ragazz- { ragazzo ragazzi

            { nuova nuove   { ragazza ragazze

---

7. The stem thus has two allomorphs: casa in the absence of P, and cas- in the presence of P -e, which may be thought of as canceling the stem-final vowel.

8. In the single instance of uomo, the stem allomorph before P -i is uomin-.

Stem-final /k/ is replaced by /č/ in some, but not all, stems before the m/p suffix -i. Thus we get, for example, amic- amici or grec- greci; but, without replacement, antic- antichi or cuoc- cuochi. There is no way to predict which stems have the replacement.

A small number of stems, most of them derived with the suffix -ist-, add a m/s allomorph -a instead of the expected -o: comunist- comunista, idiot- idiota. These are best classed with the four-form group despite the actual identity of the m/s and f/s forms.[9]

2.3.3. THE POSSESSIVES

The small set of words conventionally called "possessive adjectives" fit the testing frame used for substantives: il mio, i suoi, and so on. Five members of the set are four-form substantives: mi-, tu-, su-, nostr-, vostr-. The first three have the stem allomorphs mie-, tuo-, suo- respectively before m/p -i. The sixth member, loro, though uninflected, patterns with the rest syntactically.

English has two sets of possessives: the determiners my, your, her, and so on, and the pronouns mine, yours, hers, and so on. This classification accords with the structure of English, but the traditional labeling of Italian substantive phrases like il mio as "possessive pronouns" is a glaring example of forcing the grammar of one language into the mold of another.

There are three main points of contrast between the two possessive subsystems. The three-way semantic distinction of third-singular possession in English—his vs. her vs. its—does not exist in Italian, which has only the one third-singular stem su-. This may cease to be a problem to the student once he sees the analogy with his non-distinctive third-plural their(s). In different structures, both my and mine equate with both mio and il mio:

my uncle = mio zio	the book is mine = il libro è mio
my country = il mio paese	where's mine = dov'è il mio

This problem is discussed under the appropriate constructions. Only one English possessive, your(s), equates with the four Italian ones tu-, vostr-, Su-, Loro. Since this problem has an exact and more basic counterpart in the realm of the pronoun, we will discuss it there (¶2.4).

---

9. The stem signor- has regular G/N allomorphs except for the m/s -e. The suffix -tore- (as in the stem lavoratore-) is best described as serving to derive four-form substantives despite the fact that the masculine forms and the feminine forms pair independently like two-form substantives of the e-stem class: m/s -tore, m/p -tori; f/s -trice, f/p -trici.

2.3.4. THE CARDINALS

These constitute a special subclass of substantives, since they fit our testing frame [definite article + _____]: l'uno, i cinque, le sette. Only un- patterns like a four-form stem, although it lacks the plural forms because of its lexical incompatibility with the grammatical concept of plurality. The rest of the cardinals undergo no inflection at all. There are simple stems and derived stems. The simple stems are due, tre, quattro, cinque, sei, sette, otto, nove, dieci, venti, cento, mille. The derived stems are:

Those with -dici- affixed to the digit stem as follows, with various stem allomorphs:

Suffixed		Prefixed	
un-	undici		
due	dodici		
tre	tredici		sette → diciassette
quattro ⟩ + -dici → ⟨ quattordici		dici- + ⟨ otto → diciotto
cinque	quindici		nove → diciannove
sei	sedici		

Those with -anta suffixed to the digit stem as follows, again with stem allomorphs:

tre		trenta
quattro		quaranta
cinque		cinquanta
sei	+ -anta →	sessanta
sette		settanta
otto		ottanta
nove		novanta

All other cardinal combinations are, properly speaking, numeral phrases; they are accordingly discussed under that heading in ¶3.1.2.2. English also has cardinal numbers, as a separate part of speech. The lexical overlap with Italian is of course total.

2.3.5. THE ORDINALS

These are four-form substantives established as a subclass on the basis of their position in the substantive phrase: they fit such a testing frame as [i miei _____ tre anni]. Stems are the simple prim-, second-, terz-, quart-, quint-, sest-, settim-, ottav-, non-, decim-, prossim-, ultim-, altr-, plus those derived from cardinals by suffix-ation of -esim- : undicesim-, trentesim-, centesim-.

The lexical overlap with the English ordinal is complete, the latter set being composed of first, second, third, next, last, other, and the words derived from cardinals by suffixing -th ~ -eth : fourth, thirtieth, hundredth.

2.4. PRONOUNS

This part of speech is a restricted class of words which enjoys most of the syntactic privileges of substantive expressions except the crucial one by which the substantive itself is established, namely [definite article + _____].

Various subclasses of pronoun are determined semantically.

One subclass, the so-called personal pronouns, correlates with inflection in the verb system : io with vado, tu with vai, and so on. Its members are:

First person		me	io	noi
Second person		te	tu	voi
Third person		Lei		Loro
	m.	lui (egli)		loro
	f.	lei (ella)		
		sè		

The forms io and tu are alternants occurring as clause subjects (see ¶3.3.1.2). The forms egli and ella are by now recessive clause subjects confined to high styles; lui and lei occur freely as subjects in the colloquial standard, despite a school tradition which continues to insist unrealistically that this "is not," or "should not be," so.

English has a set of personal pronouns used in much the same ways, although it lacks any basic reflexive member and instead derives reflexive counterparts for all the members by suffixation of -self.

A difficult problem for the student is that of selection among the forms meaning you, analogous to that of the possessive equivalents for your. Only the one English pronoun equates with the four Italian ones tu, voi, Lei, Loro. The Italian situation involves two sorts of distinction not made in standard English. One is grammatical : singular tu versus plural voi and singular Lei versus plural Loro; the other is semantic, but just as compulsory : familiar tu versus formal Lei and familiar voi versus formal Loro. The student may have less difficulty with the distinction of number; various substandard regional varieties (which he knows even if he does not use them) do make a comparable distinction: <u>you</u> versus <u>you-all</u>, or <u>you</u> versus <u>youse</u>. Far more difficult is the familiar/ formal distinction, which has no parallel whatever in our students' English.

Another subclass is the demonstrative pronouns. Inflected like four-form substantives are <u>ess-</u>, <u>quest-</u>, and <u>quell-</u>.[10] With an inflection pattern <u>sui generis</u> are the somewhat archaizing three-form sets:

m/s	costui ~ questi	colui ~ quegli
f/s	costei	colei
p	costoro	coloro.

The alternants <u>questi</u> and <u>quegli</u>, obvious blends as singulars, are further restricted to reference to persons as clause subjects. Without inflection is <u>ciò</u>, referring to things only.

English has the demonstrative pronouns <u>this/these</u> and <u>that/those</u>, corresponding basically to the high-frequency Italian ones <u>quest-</u> and <u>quell-</u> respectively, but also makes much use of <u>one</u>-phrases (<u>this one</u>, <u>that one</u>, <u>the white one</u>, and so on) in situations where Italian uses the pronouns: <u>voglio questa</u> = <u>I want this one</u>.

Finally, there are the interrogative pronouns <u>chi</u>[11] (animate) and <u>che</u> (inanimate), and the relative pronouns <u>che</u> and <u>cui</u>. English has analogous pronouns: interrogative <u>who</u>, <u>what</u>, and so on; relative <u>who</u>, <u>that</u>, and so on. (See ¶3.44.)

2.5. THE DETERMINERS

The testing frame which serves to establish the part of speech we call DETERMINERS can be stated in the formula [tutt- + _____ + possessive + center]. The examples <u>tutto il mio lavoro</u>, <u>tutta una sua idea</u>, <u>tutti questi vostri vizi</u>, <u>tutte quelle loro speranze</u> demonstrate that the determiners are a class of four: the definite article <u>l-</u>, the indefinite article <u>un-</u>, the demonstrative <u>quest-</u> and <u>quell-</u> Inflectionally, all are like four-form substantives with the formula "stem + G/N," except that <u>un-</u> has no plural forms.[12]

The following paradigms of <u>un-</u>, <u>l-</u>, and <u>quell-</u> may be considered basic:

| un- { | uno | | l- { | lo | gli | | quell- { | quello | quegli |
| | una | | | la | le | | | quella | quelle |

---

10. Quell- is regular in the m/p form: <u>quelli</u> as against the determiner's m/p <u>quegli</u>.

11. Not only <u>chi</u> but also some interrogative adverbs add the derivational suffix -<u>unque</u> (<u>chiunque</u>, <u>dovunque</u>), which is of low frequency and analogous to English -<u>ever</u>. We need not return to this group.

12. In this way it is like the cardinal <u>un-</u>, with which, however, it is not to be confused; they have different syntactic privileges.

The various shorter forms (un, il, i, and so on) are alternants phonologically conditioned by their position in substantive phrases; we treat them in that connection (¶3.1.2.2).

2.6. QUANTIFIERS

The class which we label QUANTIFIERS is composed of words interrelated through two shared grammatical functions: occurrence as pre-center modifiers in substantive phrases, and occurrence as pronouns. The list is further divisible into those quantifiers which can also double as centers in substantive phrases, and those which cannot. We cite some frequently occurring members of the two subgroups:

Inflected like four-form substantives: molt-, poc-, tant-, quant-, tropp-, cert-; inflected like two-form substantives: tale, quale; uninflected: più, meno, niente;

Inflected like four-form substantives: alcun-, nessun-, ciascun-, parecchi-; uninflected: abbastanza, ogni, qualche.[13]

English also has a similar class of words (including, for example, much, many), but their lexical and distributional correspondences with the Italian quantifiers are complex and this constitutes a vexing problem for the student. We will discuss a few of the major differences under Phrase Structure (see ¶3.1.2.2).

2.7. THE DELIMITERS

The two words tutt- and ambo alone share the privilege of occurring immediately before the definite article. Tutt- inflects like a four-form substantive (tutta la città, tutti i cittadini), whereas ambo is uninflected and is lexically compatible only with plural forms (ambo le mani, ambo i piedi). Of the two delimiters, tutt- has a much broader range, since it shares the privileges of certain quantifiers: tutta Roma, così fan tutte, del tutto.

English has a like pair of delimiters, all and both, which can be established as a class by the same criterion: occurrence before the definite article (all the people, both the doors.) At the same time, these two English delimiters may occur without the definite article: all people, both doors.

2.8. ADVERBS

Traditionally, the term "adverb" has been used to designate a sort of catch-all class into which are dropped such functionally divergent words as abbastanza, quando,

---

13. As pronouns, cert- and tale- have the derived alternants certun- and talun-, with m/p and f/p forms only; ogni and qualche have ognun- and qualcun-, with m/s and f/s forms only.

anche, dunque. In the present treatment, adverbs are those words which occur chiefly as attributive complements in verb phrases (lavoriamo qui, ho mangiato bene) and less frequently in some other environments (questo qui; qui presente; ben cotto). Although adverbs may share these privileges with substantives, there remain other functions of substantives from which they are excluded—for example, clause subject. The number of adverbs is considerably swelled by the many derived from substantives with -mente. This suffix is added to the bare stem of two-form substantives (dolcemente), with loss of stem vowel after -l- (finalmente, gentilmente), and to the f/s form of four-form substantives (veramente, praticamente).

A large class of adverbs may be established for English by essentially the same criterion. The degree of lexical overlap with Italian adverbs is high: qui = here, giù = down, adesso = now, quando = when. The suffix -ly derives adverbs from adjectives, and thus corresponds functionally to Italian -mente: esattamente = exactly, brevemente = briefly. By comparison with most other parts of speech, the adverb is not a problem area for the learner.

2.9. UNIVERSALS

These are a small class including notably anche, pure, nemmeno, soltanto, quasi, traditionally lumped with the adverbs, perhaps because they are uninflected and never function as clause subjects. But neither do they function as attributive complements. They stand in a modifier-type relationship to whatever they precede, which is essentially any class of word or construction (hence the designation "universal"): anche tu, anche in Italia, anche qui, anch'io lo credo, anche se volessimo, nemmeno a me, soltanto tre o quattro, quasi tutti i libri. English has a similar class, including lexical equivalents such as only and almost. The chief problem is the position of anche (or pure) as contrasted with that of also (or too) in various types of expression.

2.10. CO-ORDINATORS

These are of two types: INTERNAL CO-ORDINATORS like e(d), o(d), nè, ma, which connect words or phrases or clauses in equivalent functions within a single sentence: ragazzi e ragazze, parlava e rideva, due o tre, nè tu nè io, bistecca di manzo e insalata verde, stanchi ma contenti, tu lo dici ma io non lo credo; EXTERNAL CO-ORDINATORS, which in opening or closing (or occasionally intervening in) a sentence serve to relate that sentence to some other sentence or to something in the situational context. Representative members of this subclass are però, oppure, dunque, comunque.

English has similar internal and external co-ordinators: internal, and, or, but; external, therefore, however. Lexical overlap is generally good, and there are few structural contrasts. In both languages, some adverbs double as external co-ordinators: allora = then.

2.11. SUBORDINATORS

These are also of two types: PREPOSITIONS, which build subordinate phrases (¶3.2); and CONJUNCTIONS, which build subordinate clauses (¶3.4). Prepositions are a large class, including the common a(d), di, da, in, con, senza, su, per. Some commonly occurring conjunctions are se, siccome, quando, che.

The division of subordinators into prepositions and conjunctions may be considered valid for English as well. Some prepositions are: of, at, in, on, with, by, up; some conjunctions are: that, if, while, although. In both languages, the lexical meaning of some prepositions is fairly elusive, and as a consequence the use of a given preposition in this or that expression cannot fail to strike the student as arbitrary. He must learn to accept and cope with this problem of selection, and not attempt to rely on lexical equivalence.

In English, a few subordinators have both functions: after the ball or after we left; before the game or before they play. In both English and Italian, some subordinators have the privilege of occurring as attributes in verb phrases: he'd never flown before; they came over to our house; andiamo fuori stasera; mettiamo su la pentola. In Italian, this is fairly limited; but in English, most prepositions function freely in this way. Present-day analysis assigns them to the verbal core itself, as a separate class of "particles," and some linguists speak of look up, take out, come in, and the like as "two-word verbs."

2.12. THE PARTICLES

These are: the NEGATIVE PARTICLE non, which functions mainly in verbal cores (¶3.1.1.1) and marginally as a universal (non tanto, non come me); and sì and no, which act characteristically as sentence constitutes but may also occur as axes in subordinate phrases (ho detto di sì, mi dicono di no) and in construction with che-clauses (sì che sono buoni, no che hai ragione).

The distribution of the English negative particle not is like that of Italian non, but we also have I guess not and the like. That of yes and no is more limited than that of sì and no; only collocations like oh, no or why, yes or yes, I am or no, you don't seem to differentiate them from interjections (¶2.13). Consequently, the learner will be slow to use sì and no in constructions like those illustrated above.

2.13. INTERJECTIONS

These are a class which, unlike particles, do not occur in construction with any other words at all. They stand at the periphery of grammatical structure, and are often phonologically peculiar (Italian /pst/ or English /š/). But they are part of language, and each language has its own stock. Sporadically they overlap in shape (both English and Italian have oh and ah), and it is certainly not unimportant for the learner to know, for example, that whereas the English implosive click, tsk, tsk, conveys disapproval or commiseration, the Italian counterpart means simply no.

PHRASE STRUCTURE | 3

3.0.

     A primary division of syntactic constructions into two types— PHRASES and CLAUSES— is valid for many languages and, by our good fortune, equally so for Italian and English. This dichotomy is, moreover, at no great remove from traditional grammatical analysis.

     Phrases are CENTERED or SUBORDINATE. A centered phrase is built around a given part of speech as CENTER, and enjoys basically the same privileges of occurrence as the part of speech occupying the center slot. For example, not only <u>pazienza</u> but also <u>tutta la pazienza che ci vuole</u> fit the frame [noi abbiamo + _____]. Since <u>pazienza</u> is a substantive, <u>tutta la pazienza che ci vuole</u> is a substantive phrase.[1] The other constituents of a centered phrase— <u>tutta</u>, <u>la</u> and <u>che ci vuole</u> in our immediate example— are MODIFIERS. Modifiers may be words, phrases, or subordinate clauses.

     A subordinate phrase is composed of a preposition followed by an expression (word or phrase) functioning as AXIS.[2]

     Clauses are PRINCIPAL or SUBORDINATE. A principal clause is built around a finite (or imperative) verb, and functions exclusively as one constituent of a sentence (the other, being an intonation contour). A subordinate clause is composed of a conjunction plus a finite clause.

---

1. Substantives and substantive phrases may be subsumed under the term "substantive expressions" or, as we prefer in the present book, "substantivals." The suffix <u>-al</u> will be used with analogous meaning also in the terms "verbal" (i.e., verb or verb phrase), "adverbial," and so on.
2. In traditional terminology "object"; but this label is best reserved for the description of verb phrase structure.

3.1. CENTERED PHRASES

Centers in Italian grammar are verbs, substantives[3] (including the subclasses of numerals and possessives), pronouns, and adverbs.

3.1.1. VERB PHRASES

Verb phrases have as constituents a CORE (functioning as center) and COMPLEMENTS of the following types: ACCUSATIVE, DATIVE, OBJECTIVE, SUBJECTIVE, and ATTRIBUTIVE. There are two types of core: SIMPLE and COMPLEX.

3.1.1.1. SIMPLE CORES

A simple core consists of a single verb in any of its inflected forms, finite or non-finite, preceded or not by the negative particle non, and accompanied or not by one or two pro-complements: guardo or non guardo or lo guardo or non lo guardo. Position of pro-complements in a simple core is determined as follows. Normally they precede a finite in any T/M and P/N (lo guardo, lo guardavi, lo guarderemo) and follow a non-finite (imperative guardalo, guardatelo, infinitive guardarlo, gerund guardandolo, participle guardatolo). By exception, they always precede the imperative plural when non is present (non lo guardate); optionally, they precede the infinitive in its replacement of the imperative singular after non (non guardarlo or, more colloquially, non lo guardare); and by exception they follow the present first plural used imperatively (guardiamolo). (For more discussion of imperatives see Clause Structure, ¶3.3.2). An infinitive with a following pro-complement attached always drops its final -e, and the -rr- of irregulars reduces to -r-: finirlo, condurlo.

Two pro-complements may occur in a single verbal core, in which instance the order of occurrence of any two is that shown in the following table.

1	2	3	4
mi ti ci_1 vi_1 gli le si	ci_2 vi_2	l-	ne

---

3. Verb phrases and substantive phrases are the two "favorite"—that is, most frequently occurring—centered constructions of the language.

Examples of the combinations indicated as possible by the table are the following:

1 + 2 : <u>mi ci lasciano, ti vi trovo, ci vi vedremo, vi ci vedrete</u>
1 + 3 : <u>me le danno, ce[4] li manderà, scrivendovelo, se l'adatta</u>
1 + 4 : <u>vattene, gliene darò, se ne accorge</u>
2 + 3 : <u>ce li manderà, ve la metto</u>
2 + 4 : <u>ce n'ho, esservene</u>

As observed in these examples, any pro-complement with final <u>-i</u> has in position 1 or 2, an allomorph in final <u>-e</u> when it precedes any pro-complement in position 3 or 4.[5]

Hard as it may be for the English-speaking student, he must be trained to react to the pro-complements as integral parts of the verbal core—as much so as the verbal inflection that signals tense-mood and the rest. He must not be permitted to regard the pro-complements as structural equivalents of the English "personal pronoun objects," which behave like any other objects within the verb phrase.

3.1.1.2. COMPLEX CORES

A complex core consists normally of two, maximally of three, verbs, plus or minus <u>non</u> (always standing first), plus or minus one or two pro-complements. The first of the verbs is an AUXILIARY, and is free to occur in any finite form or in either of two non-finite forms: the infinitive or the gerund. The form of the subsequent MAIN verb correlates with the class of auxiliary, of which there are four: PERFECTIVE, MODAL, PROGRESSIVE, and CAUSATIVE. All members of these classes can also function as main verbs.

The perfective auxiliaries are a class of two: <u>ave-</u> and <u>esse-</u>. The main verb is always in the participle form: <u>ho capito, essere arrivato</u>. Any pro-complement is attached to the auxiliary: <u>mi ha visto, non s'e alzato, avendoglielo dato</u>.

The two auxiliaries are in complementary distribution. The selection of <u>ave-</u> or <u>esse-</u> is conditioned by the main verb, in part lexically and in part grammatically.

If the main verb is one of a fairly large list of intransitives (i.e., verbs which may never have an accusative complement), many of which express motion or the like, the auxiliary is <u>esse-</u>: <u>non sei venuto, era nato, essendo giunto</u>. Robert A. Hall, Jr., in

---

4. In such instances as this, ci_1 and ci_2 (or vi_1 and vi_2) are distinguishable from one another only from the larger context in which the core is contained.

5. No exception of course is <u>gli</u> ~ <u>glie-</u>, phonologically /ʎi ~ ʎe/.

his Descriptive Italian Grammar (p. 191), gives the pertinent list of intransitive verbs as
follows: anda-, arriva-, cade-, cessa-, corre-, cresce-, diventa-, dole-, esiste-, esse-,
fuggi-, giace-, giunge-, monta-, mori-, nasce-, pare-, pari(sc)-, parti-, passa-, piace-,
piove-, resta-, rimane-, sali-, scappa-, scende-, sembra-, sorge-, sta-, torna-, usci-,
vale-, veni-, vive-, vola-.

On re-examination, examples can be found in which some of the verbs listed
by Hall as intransitives are followed by accusative complements, e.g., ho corso un
miglia, ha passato un anno in Italia. Nevertheless, the criterion for defining intransitives
as a class appears to be an adequate one.

If, regardless of the lexical class of the main verb, one of the pro-complements mi, ti, ci_1, vi_1 is present in the core and correlates with the P/N suffix of the auxiliary for reflexive reference, or if the formally reflexive si is present, the auxiliary is
esse-: mi sono alzato, non si sarà accorto.

In all other instances, the auxiliary is ave-: abbiamo finito, non averlo creduto.

The participle in a perfective core is either invariable in -o or inflected like
a four-form substantive for G/N concord. It is invariable (hanno visto, ci ha parlato) except under the following conditions.

When a pro-accusative is present in the core, whether the auxiliary is ave- or
esse-, the suffix of the participle reflects the G/N of whatever element outside the core is
replaced by the pro-accusative, with the following array of possibilities:

With ave-	With esse-
mi ha trovato	mi sono trovato
mi ha trovata	mi sono trovata
ti ha trovato	ti sei trovato
ti ha trovata	ti sei trovata
ci ha trovati	ci siamo trovati
ci ha trovate	ci siamo trovate
vi ha trovati	vi siete trovati
vi ha trovate	vi siete trovate
lo l' } ha trovato	si s' } è trovato
la l' } ha trovata	si s' } è trovata
li ha trovati	si sono trovati
le ha trovate	si sono trovate

When no pro-accusative is present in the core and the auxiliary is esse-, the suffix of the participle reflects the G/N of the subject: sono nati, è uscita, c'erano rimasti.

English has perfective cores constructed with only one auxiliary: have. As in Italian, the main verb is in the participle form: has eaten, having taken. The negative particle not ~ n't is placed between finite auxiliary and participle (had not found, haven't come); it normally precedes having or to + have (not having been, not to have loved).

Except when contracted n't is attached, forms of the English auxiliary normally have at most tertiary stress and are (except in interrogations) most often wholly unstressed. (In this respect, have as auxiliary differs from have as a main verb, always fully stressed). When unstressed, have is normally reduced to the single phoneme /v/ after a word ending in a vowel (notably the subject pronouns I, we, you, they, who) and to /əv/ elsewhere: (I)'ve quit, (we)'ve not eaten, (the boys) have left; had is normally reduced to /d/ ~ /əd/ under the same conditions: (we)'d never flown; (the boys) had left; the third singular non-past has is reduced in a pattern of allomorphs wholly identical with that of the verb form is—/z s əz/—as determined phonologically: (Jim)'s left, (it)'s been raining, (my watch) has stopped.

Reduction of unstressed forms of auxiliary have being without parallel in Italian, no aspect of the English perfective core is transferable except the basic fact that in both languages the main verb is in the participle form. But the English participle being invariable, the student is ill-prepared for the G/N inflection of the Italian participle under conditions themselves very complex. Furthermore, he has no native criterion for selecting ave- versus esse- as auxiliary. And finally, there is added to his problems the fact that he must learn to use the Italian perfective core not only as the normal equivalent of the English one but also more often than not as the equivalent of the English past tense; for example, normally both I have eaten and I ate equate with ho mangiato. This is discussed more fully under clauses in ¶3.3.1.1.[6]

The modal auxiliaries are a class of five: dove-, pote-, vole-, sape-, sole-. The main verb is always in the infinitive form: voglio vedere, non potendo servire. A pro-complement is joined either to the auxiliary (lo devo fare, doverlo fare) or to the main infinitive (devo farlo, dovere farlo), this difference in order being non-significant and stylistic; colloquial usage tends to favor attachment to the modal: me lo potete dare over potete darmelo.

Either the modal auxiliary or the main verb may form part of a perfective subcore:

---

6. Regarding what non-core elements may intervene between parts of a core in both languages, see note 63.

a	(perfective aux. + modal participle) + main infinitive		
	ha	potuto	servire

b	modal auxiliary + (perfective infinitive + main participle)		
	può	avere	servito

In cores of Type a, when the main verb is a member of the list regularly requiring esse- as the perfective auxiliary, there is a free choice of either esse- or ave- (thus siamo dovuti uscire = abbiamo dovuto uscire; participle concord with subject after esse-, but not after ave-). If the reflective si or reflexively marked mi, ti, ci_1, vi_1, are present in the modal subcore, the auxiliary is esse- and the modal participle concords; if these same reflexive pro-complements are instead attached to the main infinitive, the auxiliary is ave- and there is no concord:

> si sono dovute alzare = hanno dovuto alzarsi
> non ci siamo potuti assicurare = non abbiamo potuto assicurarci

When the auxiliary is automatically ave- a pro-accusative if present in the modal subcore causes concord, but if attached to the main infinitive it does not:

> ci hanno voluti trovare = hanno voluto trovarci
> non le ho potute capire = non ho potuto capirle

In cores of type b, choice of auxiliary and concord is determined as in regular perfective cores: non può aver(e) cominciato, dev'essere venuta. Pro-complements are always attached to the main subcore: devono averci visti, not *ci devono aver(e) visti.

English likewise has modal cores, formed with one of the modal auxiliaries followed by the general form[7] of the main verb: will see, can go. The auxiliaries are a class of five with a patterning unlike that of normal English verbs. Four of them have two forms each—present and past—whereas the fifth has only a present form:

> Present: will   shall   can   may   must
> Past   : would   should   could   might   —

These auxiliaries function as finites only. They have no general form, no participle, no gerund, and do not add the third-singular affix -s in the present. They do not combine with each other (Italian can say voglio saper(e) andare but English does not say *I will know go),

---

7. The term "infinitive" is misleading for English. The form that is traditionally called the infinitive is a phrase consisting of to plus the general form. It seems inadvisable to term go an infinitive in both he can go and he wants to go.

and they never form a perfective subcore as in the Italian <u>ho potuto andare</u>. The main verb itself may be perfective (<u>may have gone</u>) or, as we will see later, progressive or perfective-progressive (<u>should be going, should have been going</u>); but that is the extent of modal grammar, and the numerous limitations make it extremely difficult for speakers of English to control the Italian modals, which have all the morphological and syntactical properties of other verbs.

The negative particle <u>not</u> (~ <u>n't</u>) is placed between modal and main verb (<u>could not go, mustn't stop</u>). When contracted <u>n't</u> is attached, irregular formations result in four present forms:

will	/wíl/ + /nt/	=	/wównt/	won't
shall	/šǽl/ + /nt/	=	/šǽnt/	shan't
can	/kǽn/ + /nt/	=	/kǽnt/	can't
must	/mə́st/ + /nt/	=	/mə́sənt/	mustn't

Except when <u>n't</u> is attached, English modals tend to be spoken with weak stress. When they are, the vowel in <u>will, would, shall, should, can, could, must</u> becomes /ə/. In addition, <u>will, would</u> are reduced to the single phonemes /l/ and /d/ respectively after a word ending in a vowel (notably the subject pronouns <u>I, we, you, they, who</u>), as in (I)'ll quit, (I)'d quit, (who)'d know; elsewhere <u>will</u> is often reduced to /əl/, as in (John)'ll go.

The limited English modal system does not of course cover the full range of expression available to Italian modal cores. Many Italian ones have as their English counterparts constructions involving a core plus a complement containing the lexical equivalent of the main verb in the Italian core. These complements are of four types as introduced by <u>to</u> + verb (<u>wants to go, had to go, ought to go, used to go</u>); after <u>be</u> as core: adjective + <u>to</u> + verb (<u>is able to go, was supposed to go</u>) or <u>GOING</u> + <u>to</u> + verb (<u>is going to go</u>): after <u>know</u> as core: <u>how</u> + <u>to</u> + verb (<u>knows how to go</u>). In common instances of the first type, the <u>to</u> which introduces the complement is joined phonologically to the core verb, thus: <u>have</u> + <u>to</u> = /hǽftə/, <u>ought</u> + <u>to</u> = /ɔ́tə/,[8] <u>want</u> + <u>to</u> = often /wɔ́ntə/, <u>used</u> + <u>to</u> = /yúwstə/ (restricted to past tense only).

There follows here a lexico-semantic analysis of the English modals and supplementary core-plus-complement phrases, accompanied by statements and examples of normally expected Italian counterparts. We do not attempt at this point to be exhaustive about the stylistics of translation equivalence.

---

8. Like a modal except that it is followed by a <u>to</u>-verbal, <u>ought</u> is unique. Some analysts include it among the modals, along with <u>need</u> and <u>dare</u>—which two, however, are at present moving over to join the mass of ordinary verbs.

The modal will/would expresses prediction, willingness, custom.

To express prediction, Italian employs the future and conditional tenses of the main verb, with equivalences as follows:

	he will go [later]	=	andrà
	he would go [if . . .]	=	andrebbe
(he said)	he would go [later]	=	(ha detto che) sarebbe andato

With perfective main verbs, will/would expresses only prediction:

he will have gone = sarà andato

he would have gone = sarebbe andato

Willingness is normally expressed by will/would only in negative and/or interrogative cores. The Italian equivalent is vole-:

will (you) help = (Lei) vuole aiutare

he won't go [i.e., refuses] = non vuole andare

he wouldn't go [i.e., refused] = non ha voluto andare

English more often than not replaces the will/would of willingness by want + to or be + (un)willing + to, or refuse + to, obligatorily of course where the modal is excluded. Italian still uses vole-:

he wants to go = vuole andare

he won't want to go
he won't be willing to go
he'll be unwilling to go   } = non vorrà andare
he'll refuse to go

To express custom (habit, recurrence), Italian uses simply the present and imperfect tenses or (in higher styles) sole-:

(evenings) we'll read = (la sera) leggiamo or soliamo leggere

(evenings) we'd read = (la sera) leggevamo or solevamo leggere

The would of custom is often replaced by used + to:

he used to go = andava or soleva andare

The modal shall/should in formal styles may express prediction when used with first- and second-person subjects. Particularly in negative cores, the shall of prediction and the will of willingness are then in contrast:

Prediction: I shan't go; shan't you go

Willingness: I won't go; won't you go

In colloquial styles, however, <u>shall</u> is essentially limited to interrogative cores with first-person subjects, expressing a suggestion or asking for an instruction for the immediate future. The Italian equivalent is simply the present tense:

shall we go = andiamo
(what) shall I tell (him) = (cosa gli) dico

This modal also expresses obligation (fittingness, appropriateness). In special styles, such as the legislative, the present <u>shall</u> stipulates (<u>the chairman shall report</u>), but in normal colloquial styles only the past <u>should</u> has this range of meaning; it usually adds an implication of non-fulfillment. Past <u>versus</u> non-past contrast is only by perfective <u>versus</u> non-perfective main verb. The Italian equivalent is <u>dove-</u> in the conditional tense:

he should go [but he probably won't] = dovrebbe andare
he should have gone [but didn't] = avrebbe dovuto andare

When the meaning is clearly one of obligation connected with moral or social duty, English often replaces the past <u>should</u> with <u>ought + to</u>. The Italian equivalent is still the conditional of <u>dove-</u>:

he ought to go - dovrebbe andare
he ought to have gone = avrebbe dovuto andare

The modal <u>can/could</u> expresses ability, and capability (know-how).[9]
To express ability, Italian uses <u>pote-</u>, with equivalences as follows:

he can go [now] = puo andare
he can go [later] = potrà andare
he could go [if . . .] = potrebbe andare
he could have gone = avrebbe potuto andare

There are special negative instances with past <u>could</u>:

he couldn't go [<u>i.e.</u> was prevented] = non ha potuto andare
he couldn't go [<u>i.e.</u> wasn't in a position to] = non poteva andare

English often replaces the <u>can/could</u> of ability with <u>be</u> + <u>(un)able</u> + <u>to</u>, (e.g., <u>he couldn't go</u> → <u>he wasn't able to go</u> or <u>he was unable to go</u>), and it does so obligatorily in constructions which exclude the modal (<u>not being able to go</u>). Italian equivalents are also the appropriate forms of <u>pote-</u>:

---

9. In colloquial styles, it replaces <u>may/might</u> to express permission: <u>may (I) come in</u> → <u>can (I) come in</u>; see further discussion in this section.

being able to go = potendo andare

he hadn't been able to go = non aveva potuto andare

he won't be able to go = non potrà andare

To express capability, Italian uses <u>sape-</u>, with limited equivalences:

he can write = sa scrivere

he could write = sapeva scrivere

English often replaces the <u>can/could</u> of capability with <u>know</u> + <u>how</u> + <u>to</u> (e.g., <u>he can write</u> →
<u>he knows how to write</u>), and it does so obligatorily where the modal is excluded (<u>not know-
ing how to write</u> = <u>non sapendo scrivere</u>).

The modal <u>may/might</u> expresses possibility or permission. Both present <u>may</u>
and past <u>might</u> express possibility as to present or future evens; <u>might</u> indicates some
doubt that the possibility is a good one:

he may know (now) = saprà <u>or</u> può darsi che sappia

he may go (later)

he might go (though it's doubtful) } = andrà <u>or</u> può darsi che vada

A perfective main verb then expresses past possibility:

he may have gone

he might have gone } = sarà andato <u>or</u> può darsi che sia andato

To express permission, many speakers use <u>can/could</u> instead of <u>may/might</u>.
The modal does not occur with a perfective main verb in this sort of meaning. The Italian
equivalent is again <u>pote-</u>:

he may ("can") go = può andare

(I said) he might ("could") go = (ho detto che) poteva andare

In expressions of possibility, <u>may/might</u> carries at least secondary stress;
in cores expressing permission, the stress on the modal is normally weaker. Some
speakers thus have this contrast:

hè mây gó   (possibly he will)

hè mǎy gó   (he has permission to)

Since the contracted negative <u>mayn't</u> expresses only permission, an analogous contrast is
available for negative cores:

hè mây nòt gó   (possibly he won't)

hè mâyn't gó   (he doesn't have permission)

The modal <u>must</u> expresses obligation or probability. There being no tense-contrast with this modal, reference is to non-past events unless a perfective main verb is used. To express obligation, <u>must</u> is used sparingly, and only for non-past events. More often than not, moral obligation is implied. The Italian equivalent is <u>dove-</u> in the present tense:

> I must go = devo andare
>
> we must respect = dobbiamo rispettare

The modals <u>must</u> and <u>should</u> are in contrast as regards likelihood of fulfillment, as reflected in the Italian present <u>versus</u> conditional tense:

> you mustn't do it = non devi farlo
>
> you shouldn't do it = non dovresti farlo

English often replaces the <u>must</u> of obligation with <u>have</u> + <u>to</u> (more familiarly in the present <u>have got</u> + <u>to</u>), or <u>be</u> + <u>to</u>, or with <u>be</u> + <u>supposed</u> + <u>to</u>, the choice of replacement depending somewhat on the degree of external pressure implied:

I must report →
{
I have to (I've got to) report
I'm to report
I'm supposed to report
}

Replacement is of course obligatory in constructions which exclude the modal: <u>not having to report</u>. Italian equivalents are also the appropriate forms of <u>dove-</u>:

> having to go = dovendo andare
>
> he'll have to go = dovrà andare
>
> he'd have to go = dovrebbe andare
>
> he had to go = è dovuto andare ~ ha dovuto andare
>
> he'd had to go = era dovuto andare ~ aveva dovuto andare
>
> he was (supposed) to go = doveva andare

To express probability, Italian also employs <u>dove-</u>:

> he must know = deve sapere
>
> he must have known =
> {
> doveva sapere
> deve avere saputo
> }
>
> he must have gone = dev'essere andato

In expressions of probability, <u>must</u> carries at least secondary stress; in cores expressing obligation, stress on the modal is normally weaker. Some speakers thus have this contrast:

        yòu mûst stúdy   (you probably do)

        yòu mŭst stúdy   (you have to)

Since the contracted negative mustn't expresses only obligation, an analogous contrast is available for negative cores:

        yòu mûst nòt cáre   (you probably don't)

        yòu mûstn't cáre   (you're not to)

    The Italian progressive auxiliaries are a class of three: sta- (by far the most frequent), anda-, and veni-. The main verb is always in the gerund form: sto leggendo, vanno parlando. A pro-complement is joined either to the auxiliary (lo sta facendo) or to the main gerund (sta facendolo, stare facendolo), this difference in order being non-signif-icant and stylistic; as in modal cores, colloquial usage favors attachment to the auxiliary: te lo sto dicendo over sto dicendotelo.

    The progressive auxiliaries themselves do not occur in the gerund form, as can the perfective ave- or the modals (avendo detto or volendo dire, but not *stando di-cendo). In verbal cores with sequences of auxiliary + participle or infinitive + main verb, the main verb is always preceded by a preposition:

(perfective aux. + progressive participle) + a + main verb		
è	stato	a studiare
modal aux. + (progressive infinitive + a + main verb)		
deve	stare	a studiare
(modal aux. + perfective infinitive) + (progressive part. + a + main verb)		
deve	essere	stato a studiare

    English likewise has progressive cores, formed with the one auxiliary be fol-lowed by the gerund of the main verb: be going, is working. The auxiliary may itself form part of a perfective subcore, or of a modal subcore, or of both: perfective progressive have been going, modal progressive must be going, modal perfective progressive must have been going. The negative not (~ n't) is placed after the first elements in any such core.

    The relative order of auxiliary components—modal + perfective + progres-sive—is the same in both languages, with the a + main verb constructions occurring in Italian cores with sequences of more than two verbal elements.

		is	reading
	has	been	reading
must		be	reading
must	have	been	reading

		sta	leggendo
	è	stato	a leggere
deve		stare	a leggere
dev'	essere	stato	a leggere

The English-speaking student has a slight problem in that the lexical equivalent of his progressive auxiliary be, Italian esse-, is not among the Italian progressive auxiliary group. Where both languages have the main verb in the gerund form, the construction is not excessively difficult for the learner. Yet, since English does not use go or come as progressive auxiliaries, the use of anda- and veni- in this function in Italian will not come easily. If there is any transfer value in the English core + complement construction with -ing (see below, ¶ 3.2.2)—keep reading, go on reading, stop reading—it is probably nullified by the fact that many of these patterns do not equate with the Italian progressive core: stop reading = smettere di leggere.

The causative auxiliaries are a class of four: face-, lascia-, vede-, senti-. The main verb is always in the infinitive form: fa vedere, lascia stare. Causative cores differ from modal or progressive cores in that a pro-complement may never be joined to the main verb: lo fa vedere and not *fa vederlo.

A causative auxiliary may form part of a perfective modal, or progressive subcore: ha fatto vedere, deve far[10] vedere, sta facendo vedere. In perfective subcores, agreement of the causative participle is the same as that of the main-verb participles: ci siamo fatti sentire, le abbiamo lasciate vedere.

A causative core, unless it contains a pro-accusative, is inevitably followed by an accusative complement: la faccio cantare or faccio cantare + la canzone. That la canzone is indeed the accusative complement of the whole core is evident from the potential replacement of the causative core by a non-causative core containing the same main verb: faccio cantare la canzone → canto la canzone, or sto cantando la canzone. Moreover, in any of these instances la canzone can be replaced by the pro-complement la:

faccio cantare la canzone → la faccio cantare

canto la canzone → la canto

sto cantando la canzone → la sto cantando

Besides faccio cantare la canzone there exists the apparently analogous construction faccio cantare la ragazza. Yet in this instance la ragazza is not the accusative

---

10. A causative infinitive normally drops its final -e, as illustrated here.

complement of the whole core, because here <u>faccio cantare</u> cannot be replaced by <u>canto</u>—
that is, we cannot have *<u>canto la ragazza</u>. The substantive is, rather, the accusative complement of <u>faccio</u> alone, and this means that <u>faccio</u> is the main verb and not a causative
auxiliary; <u>cantare</u>, outside the core, is an objective complement (see ¶ 3.1.1.3). Despite
this difference of structuring, however, when <u>la ragazza</u> is replaced by a pro-accusative,
this <u>la</u> is of course joined to <u>faccio</u> with the result that an expression like <u>la faccio cantare</u>
in itself contains a structural ambiguity. There is none of course if the infinitive is of
the intransitive verb class—that is, a verb which does not admit of an accusative complement: <u>la faccio venire</u>. All causative cores, then, contain transitive main verbs.

      English does not have causative cores. It uses, as the content equivalent of
Italian ones, entirely different constructions composed of verb plus complement. After
most of the verbs that equate lexically with the Italian causative auxiliaries (including
<u>have</u> more frequently than <u>make</u> for <u>face-</u>), English uses object + participle, as in <u>have a</u>
<u>suit made</u>, <u>we had the things delivered</u>, <u>I'll have you arrested</u>, <u>make yourself heard</u>, <u>we</u>
<u>must make it known</u>, <u>I've seen that done</u>, <u>we heard it sung</u>. Conspicuously, the verb <u>let</u>
does not occur in this construction, so that the English equivalent of causative cores with
<u>lascia-</u> (e.g., <u>lascia scoprire la verità</u>) is at still another remove. English <u>let the truth be</u>
<u>discovered</u> is structurally the same as, say, <u>let the baby sleep</u>—that is, verb + (object +
verb phrase)—which is elsewhere the regular equivalent of Italian verb + (infinitive as objective complement + accusative complement): <u>lascia dormire il bambino</u>.

      The Italian causative core is therefore extremely difficult for the learner, not
merely because English has no such core but also because no single English construction
equates with it.

      English has one further type of complex core for which there is no counter-
part in Italian: that formed with the auxiliary <u>do</u>. Mutually exclusive with the other three
classes of auxiliary—perfective, modal, progressive—<u>do</u> is the "empty" auxiliary, a
"carrier." It takes the position of any other first auxiliary, and therefore "carries" the
tense-inflection and other signals under those conditions where a main verb in a simple
core cannot carry them. The system is fully illustrated in the following table:

	Basic	Negative	Interrogative	Contrastive-Affirmative
Present	he'll go he's gone he's going	he won't go he hasn't gone he isn't going	will he go has he gone is he going	he will go he has gone he is going
	he goes	he doesn't go[11]	does he go[11]	he does go

---

11. So also in negative-interrogative cores: <u>doesn't he go</u>, <u>didn't he go</u>.

	Basic	Negative	Interrogative	Contrastive-Affirmative
Past	he'd go	he wouldn't go	would he go	he would go
	he'd gone	he hadn't gone	had he gone	he had gone
	he was going	he wasn't going	was he going	he was going
	he went	he didn't go[11]	did he go[11]	he did go

When contracted n't is attached to do, irregular formations result:

do /dúw/ + /nt/ = /dównt/ don't

does /də́z/ + /nt/ = /də́zənt/ doesn't

did /díd/ + /nt/ = /dídənt/ didn't

The carrier do does not occur in cores where the main verb is be,[12] and only optionally where it is have—although in the latter instance American English tends to prefer use of do. Thus:

he is	→	he isn't	is he	→	he is
and not		*he doesn't be	*does he be		*he does be
he has	→	he hasn't	has he	→	he has
or:		he doesn't have	does he have		he does have

No aspect of do-cores is transferable to Italian.

3.1.1.3. COMPLEMENTS

An Italian verb phrase must have a core; it may also have, modifying the core, one or more of the following types of complement: accusative (i.e., "direct object"); dative (i.e., "indirect object"); objective; subjective (i.e., "predicate complement" etc.); attributive (i.e., "adverbial modifier").

Accusative complements modify transitive cores—cores in which the main verb is of the transitive class. A transitive verb is definable as one which may occur in a core containing the pro-accusative l- in any one of the forms la li le:[13] la conosco, la ho vista (~ l'ho vista), voglio comprarli, le faremo vendere.

---

12. Except in imperative clauses: do be careful, don't be afraid.

13. The m/s form lo does not meet the criterion because it occurs, without G/N concord to be sure, in cores where the other forms of l- do not: lo sono.

An accusative complement is in turn definable as any substantival or pronominal expression that can be replaced, in the core, by one of the pro-accusatives l- or mi ti ci, vi, si. Examples are given here with their corresponding pro-accusative replacements.

Substantivals as accusative complements:

  non conosco bene quell'uomo → non lo conosco bene

  dammi la più grande → dammela

  abbiamo visitato le città importanti → le abbiamo visitate

Pronominals as accusative complements:

  cercavano me → mi cercavano

  vogliono vedere noi due → vogliono vederci

  non ho detto ciò a nessuno — non l'ho detto a nessuno

Verbals as accusative complements, with their core always in the infinitive form:

  preferisco cominciare subito → lo preferisco

  detestiamo ascoltare queste stupidaggini → lo detestiamo

  desidera vedere il giardino → lo desidera

Subordinate clauses as accusative complements:[14]

  non so chi l'ha detto → non lo so

  mi ha chiesto se posso farlo → me l'ha chiesto

  non credevo che fosse così tardi → non lo credevo

As illustrated, the standard position for an accusative complement is following the core, with or without other complements preceding or following. When the accusative contains an interrogative or relative element, however, it precedes the core: quale dei due preferisce, che altro possiamo vedere, quanti musei hanno visitato, (tutti i libri) che ho letto.[15]

For reasons which will become apparent, comparisons with English are here withheld until the first two types of complement have been described.

---

14. Subordinate phrases introduced by di also function as accusative complements with so-called "partitive" meaning, and these are replaceable by the pro-complement ne: ho comprato delle sigarette americane → ne ho comprato. The replacement of subordinate phrases by ne goes far beyond accusative complements, and we therefore deal with it elsewhere (¶3.2.1).

15. In elevated styles, the participle in a perfective core has G/N concord with the center of a preceding accusative: quanti musei hanno visitati, tutti i libri che ho letti.

Dative complements modify a subclass of transitive cores and are definable as any subordinate phrase composed of a + substantival or pronominal axis that can be replaced, in the core, by one of the pro-datives gli or le, or by mi, ti, ci_1, vi_1, si, or by the unique loro which includes among its numerous functions that of dative complement.[16] Examples, with their corresponding pro-dative replacements:

le darò a Giovanna → gliele darò
ho scritto ieri alla mia cugina → le ho scritto ieri
possiamo offrire ai nostri clienti → possiamo offrire loro
chiedono a te → ti chiedono

As illustrated, the standard position for a dative complement is following the core; other complements may precede or follow. When both an accusative and a dative are present, either can precede the other, as determined stylistically:

hanno offerto a Mario un bel posto a Milano
　　　　　　　dative　　　accusative

devo mandare i libri al Professor Altrocchi
　　　　　accusative　　dative

When the dative contains an interrogative or relative element, however, it precedes the core: a chi hai detto questo, a quale dei tre l'ha domandato, (la persona) a cui devo il denaro.

English also has transitive verbs, which are accompanied by complements called "objects." There is, however, no formal distinction between "direct" and "indirect" object, as shown by the identical structure of I saw John and I wrote John. When some transitive verbs are accompanied by two objects—a "double-object" construction—the two are marked by position: the first as indirect, the second as direct. We say I wrote John a letter but not *I wrote a letter John. We note at once, however, that an alternate way of expressing I wrote John (a letter) is I wrote (a letter) to John, whereas a variant of we bought Paul a car is we bought a car for Paul. In the second variants, to John and for Paul are not structurally objects; they are attributive complements like to school in they sent him to school, or for a ride in we went for a ride. Nevertheless, these subordinate-phrase variants are useful in teaching Italian. If we point out to the learner that any object replaceable by a to-phrase or a for-phrase has indirect meaning and must be expressed by a dative complement in Italian, we will help him avoid constructing such un-

---

16. Loro as an accusative is replaceable by l- in the core: ho visto loro → li ho visti or le ho viste. If loro is not thus replaceable, or is not in subject or possessive function (loro sanno, la loro casa), it is a dative: ho detto loro.

grammatical phrases as *ho scritto Giovanni or even *ho scritto Giovanni una lettera.

The use of pro-complements to replace accusatives and datives in Italian constitutes a special problem for the student, since English lacks such a word class and uses personal pronouns as objects just like other (pro)nominals (I saw him, they told us). Phrases like cercano te or ho dato il pacco a lui are grammatical in Italian, but the personal pronouns so used carry phrasal stress, occur at the center of the intonation, and can only mean they're looking for YOU, I gave HIM the package. Proper use of the Italian pro-complements is one of the most difficult of tasks for the English speaker, and must be intensively drilled by means of replacements like:

> non conosco il tuo amico → non lo conosco

or responses like:

> Conosci i nostri amici? → Si, li conosco.
> Ti piace il film? → Si, mi piace.

Objective complements modify another subclass of transitive cores, including, for example, chiama-, trova-, crede-, rende-, lascia-. Substantival in form, they are not replaceable by any element in the core, and occur only in the presence of an accusative complement or of a pro-complement in the core. They equate with the accusative in the same way as a subjective complement equates with a subject (see below), the equation being marked by G/N concord. Examples:

> chiamavamo il bidello Peppino
>   Acc   Obj

> trovo il tuo amico un grande scemo
>   Acc   Obj

> lo credo molto sbagliato
> Acc   Obj

> questo renderà il lavoro più facile
>   Acc   Obj

> lascia le finestre aperte
>   Acc   Obj

The standard position for an objective complement is following the core. It normally also follows any accusative complement that may be present, although it may also precede it in order to avoid collision with a possible substantive phrase with the same ordering of elements:

> lasciate i libri aperti → lasciate aperti i libri   the books open
>   Acc   Obj   Obj   Acc

> cf. lasciate i libri aperti   the open books
>   Acc

The English equivalent of the objective complement is the double-object construction, the first being "direct" and the second "objective," as in <u>leave the windows open</u>, <u>that makes the work easier</u>, <u>we elected John captain</u>. Despite certain marginal ambiguities in English, such as <u>she called me a cad</u> versus she <u>called me a cab</u>, which the student resolves automatically, the parallelism in the two languages is such that no special difficulty will be encountered with objective complements, in any event a low-frequency construction.[17]

It might be useful to classify the infinitive <u>cantare</u> in a verb phrase like <u>faccio cantare la ragazza</u> also as an objective complement. In ¶3.1.1.2 we pointed out the structural difference between this phrase and <u>faccio cantare la canzone</u>, in which <u>faccio cantare</u> is a causative core. In the English equivalent—<u>I make (or have) the girl sing</u>—the verb <u>sing</u> may equally well be taken as an objective complement. In both languages, the verbal—infinitive in Italian, general form in English—occurs only in the presence of an "accusative," with which it equates in the same way as a subject equates with a finite verbal in a clause (<u>la ragazza canta</u> = <u>the girl sings</u>). If this analysis is accepted, the list of Italian transitive verbs admitting an objective complement must be enlarged to include <u>fa-</u>, <u>vede-</u>, and <u>senti-</u>. The order in English is the usual Direct + Objective, whereas in Italian it is typically the reverse:

ho sentito <u>uscire</u> <u>Carlo</u> = I heard <u>Charles</u> <u>go out</u>
        Obj   Acc   Acc   Obj

vedremo <u>giocare</u> <u>il tuo fratello</u> = we'll see <u>your brother</u> <u>play</u>
        Obj   Acc   Acc   Obj

An objective complement appreciably longer than the accusative one may, however, come last:

ho sentito <u>un giovanotto</u> <u>cantare una canzone popolare napoletana</u>
            Acc   Obj

In the special instance of cores with <u>fa-</u>, if the objective complement contains an embedded accusative complement of its own, the complement of <u>fa-</u> is dative and not accusative:

facevo <u>cantare la canzone</u> <u>alla ragazza</u>
        Obj   Dat

And when either the main complement or the embedded one is replaced by a pro-complement, the replacement goes in the main core:

---

17. It does need to be pointed out, however, that the Italian equivalent of <u>make</u> + objective complement is not <u>face-</u> but rather <u>rende-</u>.

facevo cantare la canzone alla ragazza = I had the girl sing the song

la facevo cantare alla ragazza   = I had the girl sing it

le facevo cantare la canzone   = I had her sing the song

gliela facevo cantare   = I had her sing it

Subjective complements modify intransitive cores, including, for example, those with esse-, sta-, anda-, veni-, sembra-, divent-, and many others. They are not generally replaceable by any element in the core, and they equate with the expressed or potential subject (see ¶3.3.1.2), the equation being marked by G/N concord in Type II substantives. Examples of subjective complements:

Substantivals:

l'altra ragazza è nostra nipote

la professoressa è diventata libera docente

loro sembrano brava gente

la macchina è un po' vecchia

sta zitto or sta zitta

Pronominals:

non è niente

sei tu, caro

si, sono io

Verbals, with the core always in the infinitive forms:[18]

volere è potere

il difficile è prendere i ladri

As illustrated, the standard position for a subjective complement is following the core; other complements may precede or follow. When the subjective complement contains an interrogative element, however, it precedes the core: chi sarà quell'uomo, qual è il Suo indirizzo.[19]

Among subjective complements belong "substantivized" participles of transitive verbs. They follow cores containing esse-, anda-, or veni-, and the phrases so built have "passive" meaning:

il libro fu scritto da un autore conosciuto

---

18. Verbals with infinitive cores may be conveniently labeled infinitivals.

19. Basically, quale = which, but it is always used (rather than che [cosa]) when asking for a selection as against a definition (cf. cos'è un indirizzo = what is an address). Since the student will tend to use che (cosa) wherever English has what is the point needs drilling.

le tessere vanno <u>sempre esibite</u>

la macchina verrà <u>ritirata</u> presto

Subjective complements in English are almost wholly analogous. Students nonetheless experience interference at four points:

The invariability of English adjectives invites failure to observe the compulsory category of G/N concord between subjective complements and subjects. Since this is a high-frequency construction, it should be drilled extensively.

In English, subjective complements are normally omitted in responses:

Is he <u>a doctor</u>?— Yes, he is.

Are they <u>very rich</u>?— No, they aren't

In Italian, they are not similarly omitted; either they are repeated or they are replaced by the pro-complement <u>lo</u>, in this instance with no G/N concord:

È <u>dottore</u>?— Sì, è <u>dottore</u>.[20]

Sono <u>cristiani</u>?— Sì, <u>lo</u> sono.

In Italian, the core verb reflects the P/N of a personal pronoun functioning as subjective complement. Hence, for example, one response to <u>chi sarà l'altro</u> would be <u>l'altro sarai tu</u>. So, also, we get:

Who is it?— It's →
- you.
- I <u>or</u> me.
- we <u>or</u> us.
- he <u>or</u> him.
- she <u>or</u> her.
- they <u>or</u> them.

Chi è?—
- Sei tu.
- Siete voi.
- Sono io.
- Siamo noi.
- È
  - lui.
  - lei.
  - Lei.
- Sono
  - loro
  - Loro.

An English phrase like <u>they were married</u>, with <u>be</u> + participle, is basically ambiguous. It may be a passive phrase, and is clearly so if expanded by an attributive <u>in</u>

---

20. In categorizing persons as to nationality or walk of life, Italian uses an unmodified substantive; cf. also <u>Paolo è italiano</u>, <u>mio padre è professore</u>. For nationality, English uses either a bare adjective (<u>he's Italian</u>, <u>they're German</u>) or a noun determined in the singular by <u>a/an</u> (<u>he's an Italian</u>, <u>they're Germans</u>). For profession or the like, English uses (<u>a/an</u> +) a noun (<u>he's a student</u>, <u>they're officers</u>), and therefore drill is needed to forestall *<u>è uno studente</u> (which is nevertheless grammatical and means something different: <u>it's a student</u>).

church or by a justice of the peace. Or it may be a non-passive parallel to they were happy, and is clearly so if expanded by an attributive only six months or the like. The Italian equivalent erano sposati contains the same sort of ambiguity. To avoid these ambiguities when necessary, English often uses the get-passive (they got married, common in colloquial styles), as Italian often uses veni- (venivano sposati or vennero sposati) or, in like instances, anda-. When, however, no agent is expressed, Italian rather more frequently than English avoids the passive phrase altogether in favor of a construction not available with this meaning in English, a reflexive core: si sposavano or si sposarono or si sono sposati. This is particularly prevalent with inanimate subjects:

English is spoken	=	si parla inglese
books are sold there	=	lî si vendono libri
it is said that . . .	=	si dice che . . .

In some instances, the preferred Italian construction is merely third plural inflection of the core, implying indefinite subject reference, and the learner must be impressed with the necessity of using this in such instances as:

I was offered a job	=	mi hanno offerto un posto
we are told that . . .	=	ci dicono che . . .

where the attempt to carry over the English passive would result in wholly ungrammatical Italian: *io fui offerto un posto, *siamo detti che . . .

Attributive complements modify cores of every type:

Adverbials:
  devono finire presto
  conosciamo molto bene l'Italia
  Carlo è qui, ma Maria è andata via
Substantivals:
  siamo stati due anni a Roma
  il castello dista qualche chilometro
  quello costa mille lire
  la carne costava molto cara
  non parlare così forte
Verbals, with the core always in the gerund form:
  sono usciti correndo
  l'appetito viene mangiando
  impariamo a parlare imitando il professore

Subordinate Phrases:

vivranno a Firenze

sono ancora in cabina

parliamo del tuo lavoro

abbia più pazienza con lui

Subordinate Clauses:

prendilo se vuoi

te lo dirò quando lo saprò

As illustrated, the standard position for an attributive complement is following the core; other complements may precede or follow. When, however, the attributive contains an interrogative or relative element, it precedes the core:

quando hai visto quel film

perchè pensi così

(lascialo) dove l'hai trovato

English attributive complements widely match Italian ones, and the learner's native habits generally do not lead him to produce ungrammatical Italian in this area. He may tend to place short attributive adverbs after instead of before other complements, saying, for example, mi piace l'Italiano molto or conosco il professor Limongelli bene, and some drill on the ordering of these complements may prove rewarding.

There is, however, one major problem. Among the attributive complements of Italian there is a subclass of expressions which are definable structurally as being replaceable, in the core, by one of the pro-attributes $ci_2 \sim vi_2$ or ne. The subclass is made up of numerous adverbials and dependent phrases which also have common lexical properties having to do with place. When used with "static" cores like esse-, they denote a location (sono qui) and are replaceable by $ci_2 \sim vi_2$ (ci sono $\sim$ vi sono); when used with "dynamic" cores like anda- or veni-, some denote a destination (vado a Roma) and are replaceable by $ci_2 \sim vi_2$ (ci vado $\sim$ vi vado), whereas others denote a provenience (vengo da Roma) and are replaceable by ne (ne vengo):

lui insegna a Bari → lui ci (∼ vi) insegna

non sono in casa → non ci (∼ vi) sono

ci vediamo lì alle quattro → ci vi vediamo alle quattro

vi vediamo lì alle quattro → vi ci vediamo alle quattro

metti il burro sulla tavola → mettici (∼ mettivi) il burro

non vogliono andare da Giorgio → non vogliono andarci (∼ andarvi)

veniamo dal Foro Romano → ne veniamo

Once again, in view of the absence of pro-complements of any sort from English, it is advisable to drill the student on replacements like:

arriveremo tardi a casa → ci arriveremo tardi

ritornano dal campo domani → ne ritornano domani

or on responses like:

Sono in camera? → No, non ci sono.

Vieni da Piazza Dante? → Si, ne vengo.[21]

In cores with esse- expressing availability or existence (c'è tempo, vi sono dei guai), the accompanying ci_2 ~ vi_2, though essential to the meaning, is not replacing any specific attributive complement. The same is true in the analogous use of vole- to express desired availability (ci vuole tempo), and in the colloquial non-significant use of ci_2 with ave- (ci ho tempo = ho tempo). The learner should have little trouble with c'è, ci sono, since it equates so neatly with his unstressed there + be.[22] He will need more pushing to control the analogue ci vuole, for which he has no close lexical equivalent, including its use of esse- in perfective cores: ci sono is to ci sono stati as ci vogliono is to ci sono voluti.

3.1.2. SUBSTANTIVE PHRASES

Substantive phrases have as constituents a CENTER—which is by definition a substantive—and MODIFIERS of the following types: delimiting, determining, possessive, ordinal, quantifying, and qualifying. Modifiers occur in fixed orders relative to one another, either pre-center or post-center. At its simplest, a substantive phrase contains a center accompanied by one modifier:

il poeta   più latte   altre due   pasta asciutta
M C   M   C   M   C   C   M

At its most complex, it may have as many as eleven modifiers, including single words of most classes, and constructions both centered and subordinate.

---

21. The pro-complement ne of course replaces some expressions in functions other than attributes. We discuss this under Subordinate Phrases, ¶ 3.2.1.

22. Yet he must be careful to differentiate this from ecco, which equates with stressed thére + be. (He may as well be told, by the way, that ecco, though uninflected and unique, is by environment and function a verb because it may be accompanied by an accusative complement: ecco le stelle → eccole, also eccomi, eccoci.

3.1.2.1. CENTERS

Every Type I substantive stem itself belongs to one of the two gender classes of the language: the masculine and the feminine. This grammatical category is semantically relevant only to the extent that it correlates with the sex of living beings named. Substantives which designate males are masculine (uomo, fratello, bue), and those which designate females are feminine (donna, sorella, vacca). Beyond this, gender-class membership shows no discernible semantic pattern. From form, gender is predictable only to a limited extent. All a-stems with plural allomorph -e are feminine (casa, settimana); all a-stems and most o-stems with plural allomorph -i are masculine (programma, libro); the few o- stems with plural allomorph -a are masculine in the singular and feminine in the plural (braccio, uovo). Otherwise, form and gender do not correlate.

In such a construction as Rodolfo torna in dicembre, the gender of the substantives Rodolfo and dicembre is grammatically irrelevant. But when a substantive occurs as a center, its gender determines the form of any modifier which is inflected for gender concord, be it determiner, delimiter, quantifier, ordinal, possessive, or Type II substantive.

The most that English has in the way of gender as a grammatical category is the obligatory three-way distinction in the singular personal pronouns: basically he/him /his for males, she/her/hers for females, it/its for neither. This is of little or no help to the student of Italian, as it gives him no basis for expecting that mano or piede has gender to begin with, or that gender causes inflectional change so as to produce la mano as against il piede. The best suggestion to the student seems to be that he acquire the habit of repeating Type I substantives in short phrases (e.g., simply definite article + center) in his learning process.

Type II substantive stems (ragazz-, grande-) have no inherent gender. When they function as centers, the four-form ones become masculine when inflected with -o -i (italiano, italiani), and feminine when inflected with -a -e (italiana, italiane). The assignment of gender, either by inflection or by mere selection, depends on: the sex of a person designated (lo zio or la zia, il poverino or la poverina); the gender of an elsewhere-located substantive (il mio or l'altro or il grande, cross-referring to, for example, some libro or some amico; la mia or l'altra or la grande, cross-referring to, for example, some macchina or some amica); arbitrary adoption of the masculine when there is no cross-reference (il bello, lo sconosciuto, il possibile).[23]

---

23. There is no possibility of a feminine counterpart such as *la possibile.

3.1.2.2. MODIFIERS

The slot of determining modifiers is filled only by the determiners. They are mutually exclusive, always pre-center, and precede any other modifier except the delimiters. The English determining modifiers take the same position relative to noun centers, and therefore present no problem of order. But a constant problem, requiring endless drill, is that of G/N agreement, which all Italian determiners show as contrasted with only the number agreement of English this/these and that/those. Some of them have alternants phonologically conditioned by whatever element of the phrase — either center or pre-center modifier — immediately follows it. The definite article l- drops its m/s suffix -o before a vowel (l'inglese, l'altro giorno) or before any consonant other than /c/, /ʒ/, /r/, /š/, or /s/ + consonant, in which instance the stem becomes il (il signore, il mio amico). It drops its m/p suffix -i before a vowel (gli inglesi = /ʎinglési/, gli altri giorni = /ʎáltri ǧórni/), whereas the stem itself goes to zero before m/p -i when followed by any consonant other than those listed above (i preti, i tuoi amici). It drops its f/s -a before a vowel (l'ora, l'unica volta). The indefinite article un- drops its m/s -o under the same conditions as does the definite article l- (un albero, un momento).[24] The demonstrative quell- has alternants matching those of the definite article and identically conditioned, so that we get quell' matching l' (l'anno, quell'anno), quel matching il (il mese, quel mese), and quei matching i (i libri, quei libri).

In English noun phrases, the use versus non-use of the definite article the provides a contrast between specific and generic reference, as in the books (are useful) versus books (are useful), (this room is for) the guests versus (this room is for) guests. This particular contrast is lacking in Italian, since substantives used in a generic sense are also modified by the definite article: wine in general — all wine, any wine — is il vino. The English speaker needs training in avoidance of the bare substantive for generic reference on the English model — *mi piace vino, for example, is ungrammatical in its use of an unmodified substantive in such a construction.

The slot of possessive modifiers is filled only by that subclass of six Type II substantives[25] which we have labeled the possessives, all of them except loro inflected for

---

24. Optional elisions of f/s -a from this and other determiners are not discussed here.

25. As centers, the possessives are limited to phrases composed of (Delimiter + Def. Art. + Center): il tuo, le nostre, tutte le mie. The G/N of the center is in cross-reference to an elsewhere-located substantive: for example, libro in the instance of il tuo, or conoscenze in the instance of le nostre. The m/p -i may have, in some contexts, its own inherent meaning of kin, followers, or the like, with no cross-reference. English of course has no analogous phrase, using instead the possessive pronouns (mine, yours) for which Italian in turn lacks counterparts.

G/N concord. They are characteristically pre-center (la nostra città, il tuo lavoro). Post-center occurrence of possessives—which then normally excludes other post-center modifiers—conveys added emphasis or emotional coloring (il piccolo paese mio, mamma mia, cosa nostra).

The outstanding fact of contrast is of course that the English and Italian possessives are members of different word classes. In English, they are determiners, occurring in mutual exclusion with the other determiners—that is, the articles and demonstratives (the house : a house : this house : my house). But in Italian, they are not mutually exclusive with the determiners. Their occurrence as the only modifier of a center, as in mio fratello or tua moglie, is restricted to common kinship phrases. In general, substantive phrases including possessives are preceded by a determiner (il nostro agente, un suo zio, queste vostre domande) or by a cardinal (tre miei studenti).

The English-speaking student will be reluctant to combine possessives with determiners, because of his native pattern of mutual exclusion which leads to such structures as a friend of yours, that voice of hers. And he will be especially slow to combine the Italian possessives with the definite article, which is a pattern of high frequency but one for which he has no transferable model.

The slot of ordinal modifiers, which comes in pre-center position between possessive modifiers and cardinal modifiers, is filled by the ordinal numbers only (¶2.3.5): la seconda strada, altri due corsi, la nostra ultima speranza, i miei primi tre mesi. The English ordinals occupy the same position (my first three months) and therefore raise no problem of order.[26]

The slot of quantifying modifiers, which comes in pre-center position between ordinal modifiers and qualifying modifiers, is filled by cardinals and quantifiers.

Examples of cardinal modifiers are: quei cinque fratelli, gli ultimi dieci anni, i vostri tre figliuoli.[27] When the only other pre-center modifier is a possessive, a cardinal by exception moves into the determiner slot, presumably by analogy with un-, which doubles as determiner and cardinal but always takes the determiner position: so un mio

---

26. The ordinals also function as centers: la terza a destra, tutti gli altri. The English ordinals are typically followed by one: the fourth one, the last ones, the other one (but also the other). They regularly function as centers in month-date phrases (the fifteenth, the thirtieth), regarding which see ¶ 2.3.5.

27. Cardinals take post-center position in some formalized phrases, such as lire duecento or ore ventitre.

cugino, and thus also tre miei cugini. The English cardinals occupy the same position (the last ten years) and therefore raise no problem of order.[28]

Cardinal phrases are made up of separate cardinal words juxtaposed in a type of unmarked construction found only within this particular subsystem: ventisette, quarantaquattro, trecentosettantacinque. The word venti and those derived by means of -anta lose their final vowel, and their stress as well, before un- and otto: ventuno, trentotto. The word mille has the allomorph mila when preceded by another cardinal: diecimila, centomila.

In these phrases, the order of components is the same in both languages, conforming as it does to arithmetic notation with the formula thousands + hundreds + tens + digits. There are nonetheless three differences: English freely alternates, for example, one thousand nine hundred with nineteen hundred, whereas Italian uses only the first type; English hundred and thousand must be preceded by something, hence by one or a if by no larger numeral, whereas in Italian they may not be preceded by un-: one hundred fifty = centocinquanta; a thousand years = mille anni; English optionally inserts and between hundreds and tens, whereas Italian never inserts e: six hundred (and) twenty = seicentoventi.

The other form-class which fills the quantifying slot, in mutual exclusion with the cardinals, is that of the quantifiers themselves: molte persone, tanta spesa, pochi soldi, troppi ostacoli, più spazio, quale negozio, niente caffè, ogni domanda, qualche parola. They do not often occur in the presence of other preceding modifiers, although such a phrase as le nostre poche speranze is perfectly grammatical. The one ordinal that accompanies them leaves its normal ordinal slot to do so, in this matching English other: molti altri motivi = many other reasons.[29]

Differences with English are manifold and perplexing. The following table shows a few selected correspondences such as the student may expect to encounter early:

Italian Quantifier	English Quantifier	English Phrase
molt-	much (+ sing.) / many (+ plur.)	a lot of / lots of
tant-		so much, as much / so many, as many

---

28. The cardinals also function as centers in both languages: i santi quattro; the big six. In Italian, they take on the G/N or an elsewhere-located substantive; thus in clock-time phrases they cross-refer to the feminine plural ore in le sei, le nove. The English equivalent is of course a different type of phrase, with the unique form o'clock.
    29. One subclass of quantifiers can also function as centers: il tale, la quale, il più.

Italian Quantifier	English Quantifier	English Phrase
quant-		how much
		how many
tropp-		too much
		too many
alcun-	some[a]	
qualche		a few
nessun-	any[b]	
qualsiasi		
nessun-		
niente	no[c]	
parecchi-	several[d]	a few / a lot of
piu	more	
meno	less (sing.)	
	fewer (plu.)	
abbastanza	enough[e]	
tale	such[f]	
quale	which	
ogni	each	
	every[g]	

The following examples illustrate correspondence with English stressed some and any: [a] (dev'esserci) qualche modo = (there must be) some way; (ci sono) alcuni problemi = (there are) some problems; (si sono fermati) qualche tempo = (they stayed) some time; (si sono fermati) qualche mese = (they stayed) some months; [b] (c'è) qualche dubbio = (is there) any doubt; (non conosco) nessun motivo = (I don't know) any reason; (accetterò) qualsiasi risposta = (I'll accept) any answer; [c] (non c'è) nessuna spiegazione = (there's) no explanation; niente latte (oggi) = no milk (today). The words some and any without stress (sŏme cígarettes, ăny mátches) do not equate with any Italian quantifier; the corresponding Italian is either no modifier at all, or a "partitive" phrase with di (see ¶3.2.1). The negatives nessun- and niente appear in semantic complementation: nessun- modifies centers indicating countable objects (nessun francobollo,[30] nessuna donna), while niente

---

30. Nessun- and alcun- drop their m/s suffix -o under the same conditions as does un-.

modifies the so-called "mass" substantives, which indicate substances not normally thought of as divisible into separate units (niente vino, niente zucchero); neither accompanies a plural center. Although qualche occurs with singular centers only, those centers are frequently "countable" substantives and in such cases the phrase has plural meaning (qualche mese, qualche parola).

[d]Examples: (abbiamo visto) parecchi film = (we saw) several (or quite a few) movies; (ripetete) più volte = (repeat) several times.

[e]English enough is free to precede or follow the center, with little if any difference in meaning (enough time = time enough, enough seats = seats enough). Italian abbastanza of course cannot follow the center.

[f]Before singular countable centers, English uses the following phrases with a/an as the second component: such a/an as in such a fool, not *such fool; but such fools, such foolishness; many a/an as a stylistic variant of many + plural center: many a time = many times. Since no such construction is available in Italian, the learner must avoid transferring the English pattern and producing *tale un- or the like. The English combinations some such, any such, no such are likewise untransferrable to Italian, in which all the quantifiers are mutually exclusive.

[g]The distinction between English each day and every day is approximately that rendered in Italian by ogni giorno versus tutti i giorni.

Qualifying modifiers are substantives, adverbs, and subordinate constructions. Type II substantives as modifiers occur either alone or in embedded phrases of which they are in turn the center. The linkage is by concord with the center: G/N for four-form substantives, and P for two-form substantives.

The function of Type II substantivals as modifiers in substantive phrases may be termed adjectival function. They occur either immediately before, or immediately after, the center (la vostra bella casa, quell'altra casa bianca), but when they themselves occur as the center of an embedded phrase (una casa molto bella, una casa più bella della nostra), that phrase normally follows the center.

The adjectival function is filled in English of course by adjectival expressions (adjectives being a part of speech in English). Since these adjectivals obligatorily precede the center of a noun phrase (white houses, a very big mistake, all those liberal thinkers), the English-speaking learner is troubled by the necessity of choosing between the two positions occupied by adjectival modifiers within the Italian substantive phrase. Correlation between meaning and position is discernible to a limited extent only. When purely differentiating and denotative, adjectivals follow the center; this is the most frequent use for a great number of them, particularly those denoting nationality, color, and the like (il governo italiano, una macchina rossa). This high-frequency pattern, being the reverse of English, runs counter to the learner's established habits. If he had no choice but post position he might the more quickly adjust to the automatic difference, but there is a choice in the adjectival modifiers which can carry connotative meanings or which describe inherent, recognized characteristics, proved experience, or the like. Thus, for example, while un generale famoso implies the co-existence of non-famous generals, on the other hand il famoso Generale Garibaldi indicates that not only is General Garibaldi recognizedly famous but also that he has no non-famous, or infamous, counterpart. With such common substantives as bell-, buon-, brutt-, brav-, pover-, nuov-, vecchi-, piccol-, grande-, the choice of position is constantly before the speaker and—if he is an English speaker—tricky because of the wide variety of semantic differences that may so be conveyed. Many phrases occur in minimal pairs, distinguished in meaning solely by position: una macchina nuova is a car that is fresh off the assembly line, while una nuova macchina is one that has been recently acquired by someone in place of another.

Phrasal stress is not normally movable in Italian from a center to a preceding modifier, as it is in English: a réd cár or a réd cár. Whichever element stands last in an Italian phrase—the center or a modifier—receives the phrasal stress: témpo brútto or brútto témpo; thus the desired placement of phrasal stress is also a factor in the selection of position in those instances where the modifier is free to take either position.

Some Type II substantives when in pre-center position have phonologically conditioned alternants: buon- loses its m/s suffix -o under the same conditions as does the article un- (buon vino); bell- has alternants exactly matching those of the demonstrative quell-, identically conditioned (un'bell' uovo, un bel pezzo, quei bei quadri);[31] sant- loses its m/s -o, and reduces its stem to san, under the same conditions as un-, when it is the sole modifier in phrases naming saints: San Pietro, San Francesco; in a few conventional phrases, grande- in its singular form is reduced to gran, phonological conditions permitting: gran parte, il gran sasso.

The adjectival function is often filled, normally in post-center position, by a substantive phrase with a Type II center. The center typically has no more than one preceding or following modifier. Pre-center modifiers are mainly quantifiers, marking no concord and therefore in the m/s form: (gente) molto brava, (bicchieri) troppo piccoli, (un libro) poco utile; and adverbials: (una risposta) così strana, (un uomo) ancora giovane,

---

31. Before m/p -i the basic stem is the expected begl- when pre-center, but normalized to bell- when post-center: begli alberi, alberi così belli.

(una lettera) ben scritta, (un lavoro) molto mal eseguito, (degli studenti) veramente
stupidi. Post-center modifiers are mainly subordinate phrases: (un appartamento) vicino
al Colosseo, (un posto) troppo pieno di gente, (una regione) molto lontana da qui; and,
marginally, adverbs or substantivals indicating dimension: (un tubo) grande così, (un
tavolo) lungo tre metri. The student has relatively little interference from English ad-
jective-phrase structure, which is generally similar (very good, too big, full of water),
but cf. two feet long, this wide with pre-center modifiers.[32]

Type I substantives as modifiers occur normally alone, but marginally in embedded phrases of which they are in turn the center.

The function of Type I substantivals as modifiers in substantive phrases may
be termed NOMINAL function. They are always immediately post-center, and mutually
exclusive with adjectival modifiers. The linkage is by selection only, the inflection of
center and modifier being mutually independent. The modifier serves to characterize,
type, or identify the center, and there are theoretically no limitations: veicoli merci, il
deposito bagagli, un gorilla femmina, Via Barberini, Piazza Sonnino, tabacco tipo ameri-
cano, il ventitre settembre. It is a type of phrase highly favored in the semi-official style
used in printed signs or the like (listino prezzi, uso ufficio). Of high frequency also is a
lexical subgroup in which the centers are substantives naming categories of persons within the structure of society—titles, professions, and the like—and the nominal modifiers
are personal names: il professore Cavicchia, la signorina Sabatini, il capitano Spavento,
il poeta Dante Alighieri. In this subgroup, the center is preceded by a determiner, typically the definite article, except when the phrase is vocative: buona sera, signor Leone.[33]

Italian Type I substantives as modifiers correspond functionally to English
nominals (i.e., nouns and noun phrases) as modifiers.

English noun phrases with nominals as modifiers include the subgroup of categorizing center + name, in the same order as Italian but never with the definite article:
President Kennedy, Professor Horatio Smith. Although other determiners occur marginally (a Mr. Clarke), the English speaker is slow to acquire the habit of using the definite
article in the high-frequency type.

---

32. This sort of substantive phrase with Type II center is also common as a
subjective complement in a verb phrase (see ¶ 3.1.1.3). With the examples given here,
compare: i bicchieri sono troppo piccoli, il libro sembra poco utile, la risposta fu così
strana, gli studenti sono veramente stupidi, l'appartamento era vicino al Colosseo, il tubo
è grande così, il tavolo è lungo tre metri.
33. This example shows also the conventional dropping of m/s -e from signor-
in this construction.

Of much wider significance, however, is the unlimited use in English of phrases with a noun center preceded by a nominal modifier (lace curtains, a gold watch, the Christmas holidays), including modifiers with possessive inflection (John's parents, the government's decision, the horse's mouth). Innumerable two-component noun phrases of this sort are further unified by a primary + tertiary stress pattern (drúg stòre, dáiry fàrm, hóusekèeper), which often constitute a type of "center phrase" in larger noun phrases such as the corner drug store. We recall that in Italian no nominal modifier ever precedes a center. In a minority of instances, the Italian equivalent of an English noun + center may be simply the above-described center + nominal modifier: the Fiat Agency = l'Agenzia Fiat, or price list = listino prezzi—but observe that the Italian attribute may be pluralized.[34] In the vast majority of cases, however, the corresponding Italian phrase is one consisting of center + subordinate phrase, which we discuss in ¶3.2.1.

A small number of lone adverbs may immediately follow a center, in mutual exclusion with adjectival or nominal modifiers: il giorno dopo, i denti davanti, un amore così, questa macchina qui, quel palazzo lì. The "place" adverbs qui qua lì là occur only when there is a demonstrative determiner, qui qua going with quest- and lì là with quell-. In English, adverbials follow centers much more freely: all the students together, the week before, the waiters here, those planes up there, the weather out here. The student may therefore need to be restrained from using the construction too freely and coining expressions like *i camerieri qui.

Subordinate phrases, the internal structure of which is described in ¶3.2, invariably follow the center or any post-center modifier except a subordinate clause in both Italian and English. They are of high frequency in both languages. Quantities of them are analogous in the two languages, and constitute no problem: una bottiglia di vino = a bottle of wine, or la città di Roma = the city of Rome. But Italian subordinate-phrase modifiers also parallel many English nominals (tabacco da pipa = pipe tobacco), including all instances where the English modifier carries possessive inflection: il nome di quel signore = that gentleman's name; il marito di mia sorella = my sister's husband. These pairs also illustrate how English possessive modifiers (including such phrases as my sister's) exclude and replace any determining modifier, whereas in the Italian counterparts a determiner occurs as expected. The English-speaking learner must be drilled in supplying it.

---

34. Month dates also follow this pattern in Italian: (il primo febbraio, il quindici luglio), with the cardinal (or ordinal in the one instance of primo) as center and the month name as nominal modifier. Drill on this is in order, since English resorts to a completely different construction: February first or the first of February.

Subordinate clauses, the internal structure of which is described in ¶3.4, invariably follow all other qualifying modifiers in both Italian and English. In Italian, either they are introduced by the conjunction che (la speranza che tutto andrà bene) or they contain a relative word (le parole che seguono, il signore da cui andiamo, il paese dove sono nato). English subordinate-clause modifiers are essentially parallel, being introduced by the conjunction that (the hope that all will go well) or containing a relative word (the letter which follows, the town where I was born).

3.1.3. PRONOUN PHRASES

The center is a personal pronoun, a demonstrative pronoun, or un-. When it is a personal pronoun, modifiers may be adjectival (io stesso, noi sole), nominal (voi studenti, noi donne), cardinal (loro tre), or subordinate (Loro dell'America, voi che entrate). The only pre-center modifier is the delimiter tutt-: tutti voi, tutte queste. When the center is a demonstrative pronoun, modifiers are mainly adjectival: quello magro, queste più grosse. The pronoun un- also has adjectival modifiers: uno rosso, una più pulita. The masculine forms of un- and quell- show formal contrast between pronominal centers and these same words as determiners, but the contrast is neutralized in the feminine forms and in quest-:

	Centers	Determiners
contrast	uno inglese	un inglese
	quello giovane	quel giovane
	quelli neri	quei neri
no contrast	una italiana	una italiana
	quelle vecchie	quelle vecchie
	questo povero	questo povero

English always makes the contrast, but by a different means—often by a one phrase versus a noun:

an Italian one	an Italian
those red ones	those reds

The demonstratives may be followed by essentially the same adverbial modifiers as may substantive centers, with the same limitations (see ¶3.1.2.2): questo qui, quella là, quelli davanti.

The demonstratives, as well as cardinals and quantifiers functioning as pronouns, are often modified by subordinate phrases or clauses:

quelli del nord	quelli che vuoi
uno dei nostri	una che ti piaccia
cinque dei migliori	tre che mancano
molti di questi negozi	pochi che lo sappiano
nessuno dei pezzi	qualcuno che possa farlo

English uses essentially the same constructions: those in the north, one of the best, none that I know of, someone who cares.

3.1.4. ADVERB PHRASES

The center is by definition an adverb, and typically has no more than one preceding or following modifier. Pre-center modifiers are mainly quantifiers, marking no concord (molto bene, abbastanza male) and adverbs (così lentamente). Phrases with post-center modifiers are limited mainly to place expressions such as qui dentro, lì sopra, lassù (= la + su), quaggiù (= qua + giù), in which the modifiers are also adverbs.

English adverb phrases have mainly pre-center modifiers (very well, rather weakly), and thus run counter to the Italian type of qui dentro: in here, out there, down under, up above.

3.2. SUBORDINATE PHRASES

These are fixed-order constructions of only two constituents: a SUBORDINATOR, and an AXIS. The subordinator slot is filled by a preposition or equivalent phrase; the axis slot is filled mainly by substantivals (in casa) and verbals (per arrivare).[35]

Italian and English subordinate-phrase structure is fundamentally the same, but there are numerous divergences of function. We will shortly consider substantival and verbal axes under separate headings.

In both languages, some combinations of words, the last one a preposition, fill the subordinator slot like a lone preposition: Italian dentro del tempio, prima di me, al di là del Colosseo, a causa della pioggia, da parte del signor Mattu, dietro alla casa, davanti al Duomo, quanto a lui; English out of sight, because of fear, in front of the house, as for you. Few of them overlap, and the Italian ones must simply be learned as so much

---

35. Not infrequently also by pronominals (per me, da Lei); and marginally by other parts of speech (per adesso). Noteworthy in passing are certain oddments not matched in English. The phrases di più and di meno correspond to more and less in such expressions as lavora di più (as against non lavorare più); tre sedie di più, cento lire di meno. Phrases like di qua, di là, di sotto, di sopra, with adverbial axes, are also fairly common: andiamo di là, il piano di sotto.

vocabulary. Most of them are composed of some non-preposition plus di or a; but it must also be pointed out that by analogy with phrases like prima di, the prepositions dopo, contro, su, sotto, sopra, senza, and fuori also add di before some axes, notably pronominal ones: dopo di me, su di esse, senza di te.

3.2.1. SUBSTANTIVALS AS AXES

So many of these high-frequency phrases overlap in the two languages that it is superfluous to give random examples. The student has one morphophonemic problem. Before substantive phrases headed by the definite article, six common monosyllabic prepositions have allomorphs joined phonologically to the article:

a	a$^+$	(allo zio, al gatto, alla volta, agli altri, ai miei, alle otto)
di	de$^+$	(dello stato, della casa)
da	da$^+$	
in	ne$^+$	
su	su$^+$	
con	co$^{+\,36}$	

The symbol $^+$ (after Hall) indicates doubling of the initial consonant of the article, including of course that of gli (/aʎʎi, neʎʎi/).

Phrases of di plus a substantival determined by the definite article constitute, in some environments, so-called "partitive" expressions which have no counterpart in English. They occur with mass substantives in the singular and countable substantives in the plural, and equate with English nominals modified by unstressed some/any or unmodified:

del pane = (some, any) bread

delle buste bianche = (some, any) white envelopes

Unlike other subordinate phrases, this di- partitive may function as a clause subject: (sono arrivati dei bei fiori, ci sono delle cose interessanti), or as an accusative complement in a verb phrase. In the latter instance,[37] it is replaceable by the pro-complement ne:

avete del tabacco olandese → ne avete

---

36. The present tendency is to use this allomorph before il and i only: col tempo or coi piedi, but con la mano.

37. As also with subjects of c'è, ci sono: ci sono delle cose interessanti → ce ne sono.

devo comprare <u>dei francobolli</u> → devo comprar<u>ne</u>[38]

The replacement of a <u>di</u>-phrase by <u>ne</u> in the core is not limited to the partitive. Any <u>di</u>-phrase embedded (as modifier) within a pronoun phrase functioning as accusative complement is replaceable by <u>ne</u> in the core:

conosco molti <u>degli studenti</u> → <u>ne</u> conosco molti

ho visto due <u>di quelle macchine</u> → <u>ne</u> ho visto due

non hanno visitato vessuno <u>dei musei</u> → non <u>ne</u> hanno visitato nessuno

By a still further extension, substantive centers modified by quantifiers or cardinals in accusative complements are replaceable by <u>ne</u> even when no <u>di</u>-phrase is present:

ho letto qualche libro → <u>ne</u> ho letto qualcuno

mi dia tre scatole → me <u>ne</u> dia tre

As with other pro-complements, the student should be drilled in the use of <u>ne</u> in such replacements, as well as in responses to questions with <u>quant-</u>:

Quante di quelle chiese hanno visitate?— Ne abbiamo viste poche.

Quanti pacchetti devo comprare?— Còmprane parecchi.

Quanti anni ha Lei?— Ne ho ventiquattro.

Quanti soldati c'erano?— Ce n'erano cinque mila.

Quanto latte c'è?— Ce n'e un litro.

3.2.2. VERBALS AS AXES

The core of an Italian verbal functioning as axis is always in the infinitive form: <u>da fare</u>, <u>per andarsene</u>, <u>senza ringraziarci</u>, <u>a spendere dei soldi</u>. The learner has thorny problems here. In English, all verbal axes of prepositions take the <u>ing</u>-form (<u>of working</u>, <u>to drinking</u>,[39] <u>for traveling</u>, <u>without trying</u>), and there is therefore constant temptation to use the formally analogous gerund, or <u>ndo</u>-form, of Italian in any axis.[40] Where a

---

38. If the partitive construction were compulsory in Italian, it would constitute a much greater hurdle for the student. But, at least as an accusative complement, it is in free stylistic variation with an undetermined substantival: <u>devo comprare francobolli</u> is equally grammatical. The replacement is still <u>ne</u>, however: <u>Hai comprato sigarette?— Sì, ne ho comprato</u>.

39. The <u>to</u> which precedes the general form of an English verb (<u>to drink</u>, <u>to travel</u>) is of course not a preposition at all; it belongs to the subordinator class, but is structurally unique and devoid of all except grammatical meaning.

40. On the other hand, the gerund is indeed called for, but with no preposition, in certain instances where English has <u>by</u> or <u>through</u> or <u>while</u> plus -ing: <u>by working all night</u> = <u>lavorando tutta la notte</u>; <u>while waiting for George</u> = <u>aspettando Giorgio</u>.

choice of preposition must be made, the corresponding English expressions may consist merely of a _to_-verbal, thus furnishing no lexical clue to the selection:

> the need to eat = la necessità di mangiare
> very glad to see you = molto lieto di vederLa
> I have nothing to do = non ho niente da fare
> I said it to warn them = l'ho detto per avvertirli
> we were about to go = stavamo per andare
> these are to be thrown away = questi sono da buttar via[41]

In attributive complements where the "doer" of the infinitival action is identified by the subject of the core, the lexical determinant of the preposition to be used resides in the core verb rather than in the preposition itself: in _prometto di farlo, di_ is determined by _promette-_. English shows a miscellany of correspondences, mainly _to_-verbals or subordinate clauses:

> giura di dire tutta la verità = swear to tell the whole truth
> ha tentato di trovarne = she tried to find some
> decisero di partire = they decided to leave
> dichiaro di aver pagato = I declare that I have paid
> non credo di conoscerla = I don't believe that I know her
> sono andati a comprare vino = they've gone to buy wine
> comincio a capire = I begin to understand
> sto imparando a giocare = I'm learning to play
> non riesce a imparare = he doesn't succeed in learning
> avevano da servire = they had to serve

Conversely, some Italian correspondences with English TO-verbals are not subordinate phrases at all. Selected examples:

> he wants to study = vuole studiare (modal core)
> he likes to study = gli piace studiare (infinitival as subject)
> he prefers to study = preferisce studiare ⎫
> he hates to study[42] = detesta studiare ⎬ (infinitival as accusative)

---

41. The avoidance of a passive construction in Italian is of course an extra hazard here.

42. Alternative English constructions with _-ing_ are an extra problem here, so that preventives against *_preferisce studiando_, *_detesta studiando_, *_smette studiando_ are also in order (but cf. _he learns by studying_ = _impara studiando_).

In attributive complements where the "doer" of the infinitival action is identified by an accusative or dative, the lexical determinant of the preposition—as between di and a—resides in the core verb. English has a to-verbal:

ti vieto di ridere = I forbid you to laugh
preghiamo i clienti di iscriversi = we beg the clients to register
chiederò a Maria di cantare = I'll ask Mary to sing
domanda agli altri di aspettare qui = ask the others to wait here
chi ti ha detto di smettere = who told you to stop
mi hanno invitato a cenare = they have invited me to dine
aiutami a finire il lavoro = help me to finish the work
non ci insegnano a parlarlo = they don't teach us to speak it

Conversely, the Italian correspondence with one high frequency English to-verbal in the presence of an accusative is a suborinate clause with subjunctive core rather than a subordinate phrase:

they want their friends to know = vogliono che i loro amici sappiano

Such instances are discussed further in the section on Subordinate Clauses (¶3.4.8).

3.3. CLAUSES

The favorite construction in both Italian and English, as one constituent of a sentence,[43] is the CLAUSE. In both languages the potential constituents of a clause are a SUBJECT, a PREDICATE, and one or more MODIFIERS. And in both languages, clauses are divided into two types: FINITE and IMPERATIVE. Every Italian clause, finite or imperative, has a predicate, but may or may not have a subject. In English, finite clauses have both a subject and a predicate; imperative clauses have a predicate, and may—but typically do not—have the subject you. We first take up finite clauses as the more frequent as well as the more problem-laden for the English speaker. After continuing with imperative clauses, we devote a section to modifiers, which in both languages are optional constituents of either type of clause. Finally, we give special consideration to subordinate clauses.

3.3.1. FINITE CLAUSES

Finite clauses contain a wide variety of inflected forms in both predicate and subject slots.

---

43. The other is an intonation contour.

3.3.1.1. PREDICATES

The predicate slot is filled, as in English, by a verbal with the core in any finite form. Selection of the P/N inflection is conditioned by factors outside the core itself: it shows P/N concord with the subject if there is one (io lavoro, essi lavorano), and it identifies the person and number of the "doer" of the action if there is no subject (lavoro can only mean I work, lavorano only they work, whoever they are)—this being deducible only from the linguistic or non-linguistic context of the sentence. Selection of the T/M inflection, on the other hand, is conditioned only when the clause is subordinate, and then not always; otherwise it is unconditioned, and the learner faces problems because his English repertory of tenses is smaller. The Italian tense-mood system may be illustrated:

$$\leftarrow \text{mood} \rightarrow$$

		present	present subjunctive
↑ tense ↓	future		
	preterit	imperfect	past subjunctive
	conditional		

It is not difficult for the student to differentiate past from present in a general way, or indeed to equate the future tense with will-cores and the conditional with would-cores. Beyond this, however, he gets no pointers from English as to when the present subjunctive must replace either the present or the future, or when the past subjunctive must take over for the preterit, imperfect, or conditional. In finite clauses, the subjunctive problem arises almost exclusively when they are subordinate, and we will best deal with it under that heading. This leaves the past-tense problem of the preterit versus imperfect contrast—the aspect under which a past action is viewed and consequently reported.

It is of little avail to explain to the student at length the uses of the preterit and imperfect tenses. He can be told how the preterit means that the action is viewed in its entirety and unrelated to other events, and how the imperfect reports an action looked back in upon as it either unfolded or recurred as background for other events; but the choice is ultimately of a lexical order, as seen by the following correspondences:

we met them (habitually) ——————————— li incontravamo ⎫
                                      ————— li incontrammo ⎭

we met them (an event) ————————— li conoscemmo ⎫
                                    ————— li conoscevamo ⎭

we knew them ————————————— li sapevamo ⎫
we found them out ——————————— li sapemmo ⎭

he didn't want to go————————————— non è voluto andare

he wouldn't (i.e., refused to) go————————— non volle andare

Neither does it help the student to know that in present-day standard Italian the preterit is a recessive tense, kept alive mainly for use in formal narrative. For it is not the preterit-versus-imperfect contrast that is disappearing as a consequence, but a different one—which the English speaker makes without difficulty—that of preterit <u>versus</u> perfective present:

we have seen it ——————————————— l'abbiamo visto

we saw it ——————————————— (lo vedemmo)

——————————————— lo vedevamo

If taught to avoid the preterit for ordinary purposes, the student is still obliged to make the hard choice between <u>l'abbiamo visto</u> and <u>lo vedevamo</u> for <u>we saw it</u>.[44]

3.3.1.2. SUBJECTS

This slot is most frequently filled in Italian by a substantival or pronominal, as in English by a nominal or pronominal. In both languages, it is sometimes filled by a subordinate clause, also, occasionally, in Italian by an infinitival (<u>è difficile lavorare</u>) and in English by a <u>to</u>-verbal (<u>it is hard to work</u>).

In Italian, the order of subject and predicate is for the most part free. Unless the subject contains an interrogative word (<u>chi te l'ha chiesto</u>), or unless it is an infinitival (<u>è impossibile finire oggi</u>) or a subordinate clause (<u>è vero che vengono stasera</u>), it may come either before or after the predicate: <u>il mio collega era andato in Sicilia</u> or <u>era andato in Sicilia il mio collega</u>—the choice of order often being stylistic. It is well to remind the student, however, that Italian sentence stress typically falls on the second constituent of a clause, whereas in English it freely shifts. This is a factor in the selection of position for the Italian subject in those instances where it is free to take either position:

the Rossínis have arríved in Róme ⎤
sono arriváti a Róma i Rossíni ⎦ a statement about who has arrived

the Rossínis have arríved in Róme ⎤
i Rossíni sono arriváti a Róma ⎦ a statement about what the Rossinis have done

---

44. Conversely, for the Italian learner of English, the obsolescence of the preterit leaves the choice between <u>we saw it</u> and <u>we have seen it</u> for <u>l'abbiamo visto</u> a major hurdle. If, however, he retains some familiarity with use of the preterit, this can be exploited by directing him to say <u>we saw it</u> when <u>l'abbiamo visto</u> is replaceable by <u>lo vedemmo</u>.

The student will of course be slow to put the subject second, since English subject-predicate order is essentially fixed. The marginal reversal in here comes the bus can hardly serve as a productive model for predicate + subject. The splitting of the core by the subject in interrogative transforms (has John arrived, can you tell me) has no regular counterpart in Italian, unless some analogy can be drawn between this and the occasional intervention of short (chiefly pronominal) subjects between the core and one or another complement: sai tu la ragione, ha visto Lei il Palazzo Antici Mattei.[45]

A serious interference may result—at least in early stages—from the obligatory occurrence of some form of subject in any English finite clause. In Italian, any finite clause with subject and predicate is potentially reducible to the predicate alone, with the core marking at least the P/N of the "doer":

i Rossini sono arrivati a Roma → sono arrivati a Roma

The subject of the English equivalent of the reduced clause is of course they, and it precisely in the realm of personal pronoun subjects that the student will most readily err. He will feel the need to express personal pronoun subjects in Italian and say, for example, io non vado to mean I'm not going—whereas what he is actually saying means (as for me) I'm not going (although somebody else may be). If he extends the English model so far as to say *lui non va perchè lui non può, he has of course stepped over the line of actual grammaticality.

In English clauses like it is hard to do this or it is true that they do this, the average learner is probably unaware that the actual subject comes second and that it is merely a dummy filler of the regular subject slot. In Italian equivalents, he will naturally achieve the proper order, but he must still know that it can have no counterpart.[46]

Some Italian clauses of predicate only, with the core conventionally in the third singular, have not even a potential subject: sta piovendo, fa freddo. In a minimal contrast between a third-singular clause which does have a potential subject and one which does not, the second type is marked by the function word si in the core:

dove entra	(potential subject lui, Carla, etc.)
dove si entra	(no potential subject)

---

45. But not *ha Lei visto.
46. He will not realize that it is hard to do this and it (= this) is hard to do are totally different constructions, their analogues kept apart in Italian by the use of a da-phrase for the second:

Pred. + Subj.   è difficile fare questo
Pred. only   (≠)   è difficile da fare

There is of course no English counterpart to si.[47] The student must learn to use it where English has an "indefinite" subject like one, you, they, or a passive.

3.3.2. IMPERATIVE CLAUSES

The predicate slot is filled by a verbal with a simple core in the imperative singular or plural (guarda, non guardare: guardate, non guardate) or in the present subjunctive third singular, third plural, or first plural (guardi; guardino; guardiamo).[48] The imperative forms are used in "commands" to persons whom the speaker is accustomed to addressing as tu or voi, and only these pronouns (or phrases containing one of them, like voi stessi or tu e lui) may occur as subjects: scrivi tu la lettera, non ci entrare tu solo, pensateci voi due. The present subjunctive is used in "commands": to persons addressed as Lei or Loro, with only these pronouns (or phrases containing one of them) occurring as subjects—ci pensi Lei stesso, me lo lasci Lei, aspettino anche Loro un attimo; to a group including the speaker, with only noi (or a phrase containing it, or a co-ordination containing io) occurring as subject—badiamo noi a quello, facciamolo tu ed io.

In English imperative clauses, the verb is in the general form, and only you can occur as subject (you find it, don't you do that). In both languages, imperative clauses with no subject are by far the more frequent: dormi bene, s'accomodi pure, vediamo che altro c'è; sleep well, come in, let's see what else there is. The only problem, when for contrastive emphasis a subject does occur, is that of order: in Italian the subject normally follows the core, in English it precedes—fallo tu se puoi = you do it if you can. Once the student finds that there is no Italian equivalent for let's, he adjusts readily enough to first-plural inflection of the core.

3.3.3. CLAUSE MODIFIERS

In both Italian and English, the function of clause modifier is filled by the same form classes that fill the attributive complement slot in verb phrases: adverbials, substantivals, verbals, subordinate phrases, and subordinate clauses. They are distinguished from attributive complements by criteria of position and intonation, standing first in a clause, under a separate intonational contour or not:

domani mattina si sapranno i risultati dell'elezione

spaventato, il povero Alfredo non potè muoversi

---

47. Although this si is historically the same as the reflexive pro-complement si, the two are no longer the same structurally: cf. lo si dice with se lo dice.
48. The position of pro-complements relative to core verbs in imperative clauses has been discussed in ¶3.1.1.1.

essendo qui vicino, volevo salutarLa

dovunque siano andati, li troveremo di certo

in questo caso non vale la pena

siccome il principale è fuori Roma, Lei dovrà aspettare

quando sente qualcosa di nuovo, me lo dica

se piove domani, bisognerà spostare la gita

or last in a clause, often following an attributive complement in the predicate, and always under a separate intonation contour:

ho letto il libro l'anno scorso, mentre ero ammalato

la nave arrivò il quattordici settembre, alle cinque del mattino

è un peccato, perchè mi piaceva molto

i giovanotti restarono fuori, chiacchierando e ridendo

ci riuniamo stasera, dopo il concerto

3.4. SUBORDINATE CLAUSES

In both Italian and English, these function as subjects in larger clauses; as accusative complements in verb phrases; as attributive complements in verb phrases or as clause modifiers; as modifiers in centered phrases, chiefly substantival ones. And in both languages, they are constituted in either of the same two ways: by a conjunction plus a clause in that order; or by a clause containing an interrogative or relative word with dual function, serving to subordinate the clause and at the same time filling a given slot within it.

All subordinate clauses are finite, with the core in any inflected form. Selection of the Italian P/N inflection has no special limitations; but selection of the T/M inflection is variously conditioned by a series of factors operating in subordinate clauses only, and constituting a major complex of difficulties for the English speaker. With reference to our diagram of the tense/mood system on p. 69, selection as to MOOD (the right half of the box as against the left) is sometimes automatically conditioned by factors outside the subordinate clause, sometimes by the conjunction itself, sometimes not at all; and that selection as to TENSE (below the center line of the box as against above it) is often, though by no means always, governed by the principle of tense sequence.

We will treat subordinate clauses under their various functions.

3.4.1. AS SUBJECTS IN CLAUSES

These are clauses subordinated by the conjunction che, and will be hereinafter referred to as che-clauses. They follow the predicate:

risulta che ha ragione Lei

è vero che siamo felici

sembra perfettamente chiaro che ti hanno ingannato

When the principal core contains one of a smallish lexical group of "affective" verbs expressing an influence either desired or realized—for example, occorre-, bisogna-, conveni-—or a verb expressing uncertainty or emotional involvement on the part of the doer—for example, pare-, piace-—the che core is automatically subjunctive in mood:

occorre che vi presentiate domani

bisognerà che me lo dica, però

mi pare che ci sia stato uno sbaglio

ti piace che abbia smesso di fumare

Le dispiace che io pensi così

Negative cores with esse- or risulta-, either with or without a subjective complement such as ver-, cert-, chiar-, evidente-, also bring on an automatic subjunctive:

non è che Glielo possa promettere

non risulterà che ci conoscano

non è chiaro che ci sia altro da fare

In the presence of a subjective complement expressing influence, denial, uncertainty, or emotion—typically but not obligatorily after cores with esse-—the che core is automatically subjunctive:

sarà necessario che gli scriva

è impossibile che arrivino così presto

sembra poco probabile che ce lo concedano

(è un) peccato che tu non mi creda mai

3.4.2. AS ACCUSATIVE COMPLEMENTS IN VERB PHRASES

These are che clauses, and interrogative clauses—clauses in which any slot within the subject or the predicate is occupied by an interrogative word.

che clauses:

sappiamo che lui non può venire

ripeto che tutto sarà inutile

When the principal core contains an affective verb—vole-, desidera-, preferi(sc)-, suggeri(sc)-, insiste-—the che core is automatically subjunctive in mood:

> vuoi che rimanga con te
>
> Lei desidera che incarti il libro
>
> preferiranno che non si venda più niente

For those students who would say, they prefer that nothing more be sold (of whom there are increasingly few nowadays), the parallel with the English recessive subjunctive can be pointed out as regards this group of verbs. But of course by far the commonest of them is vole-, and English want is followed instead by a to-verbal.[49] The optional omission of English that in certain environments (we know he can't come) may tempt the beginner to omit che; even though this is possible in certain styles, he should be discouraged from doing so.

When the principal core contains a verb expressing uncertainty or fear— crede-, teme-, or non + pensa-—the che core is likewise automatically subjunctive:

> credo che sia troppo tardi
>
> temo che loro abbiano ragione
>
> non penso che tu scriva proprio bene

After main cores containing spera- in a first person form, or verbs of alleging such as dice- or dichiara- not in a first-person form, the mood of the che core actually reflects that of the speaker:

> spero che gli affari andranno meglio   spero che gli affari vadano meglio
>
> [and this seems to me likely]   [and I strongly desire it]
>
> dicono che l'autostrada è gia aperta   dicono che l'autostrada sia già aperta
>
> [and I accept this statement as true]   [but I doubt their accuracy]

The main cores of interrogative clauses typically contain dice-, domanda-, sape-, vede-, capi(sc)-, and the like:

> Lei puo dirmi chi è quel signore
>
> domanda ai ragazzi quali di loro possono andare
>
> sai quando partono e dove vanno
>
> dimmi che genere di libro vuoi leggere

---

49. English wish + subordinate clause presents a very special problem:
> I wish (that) I knew [but I don't] = vorrei sapere (modal core in condi-
> tional)
> I wish (that) you were here [but you aren't] = vorrei che fossi qui (con-
> ditional of vole- plus past subjunctive)

> hai capito <u>perchè non voglio farlo</u>
> gli ho domandato <u>se[50] tutto va bene</u>

When <u>sape-</u>, <u>capi(sc)-</u>, <u>vede-</u>, or the like is preceded by <u>non</u>, thus removing the doer's perception of the reality involved, the subordinate core is automatically subjunctive:

> non so <u>che ora sia</u>
> non capiamo <u>perchè sia così</u>
> non sappiamo <u>se per caso dicano bene</u>

3.4.3. AS ATTRIBUTIVE COMPLEMENTS IN VERB PHRASES, OR AS CLAUSE-MODIFIERS

These are clauses subordinated by various conjunctions, particularly <u>se</u>, <u>quando</u>, <u>come</u>, <u>dove</u>, <u>mentre</u>. Also some combinations of words, the last one usually <u>che</u>, fill the slot of a lone conjunction: <u>prima che</u>, <u>benchè</u>. English has more one-word conjunctions than Italian (<u>although</u>, <u>before</u>, <u>because</u>), some of which double as other parts of speech—for example, <u>before</u>, an adverb and a preposition as well as a conjunction. Some examples of attributive complements:

> finiranno il loro compito <u>se potranno</u>[51]
> te lo darò <u>quando ritornerò</u>[51] da Torino
> metta quella roba <u>dove vuole</u>
> cerca di farlo <u>come lo faccio io</u>

After one group of subordinators, common among which are <u>benchè</u> ~ <u>sebbene</u>, <u>purchè</u>, <u>senza che</u>, <u>a meno che</u>, <u>caso mai</u>, use of the subjunctive is automatic:

> <u>benchè</u> (or <u>sebbene</u>) <u>non ti piaccia</u>, dovrai farlo
> lo scriverà volentieri <u>purchè glielo paghino</u>
> esci <u>senza che ti veda nessuno</u>

After another group of subordinators, common among which are <u>perche</u>, <u>prima che</u>, <u>dopo che</u>, <u>di modo che</u>, the subjunctive is selected to express anticipation, including purpose and the like. Compare:

---

50. This <u>se</u> is the interrogative conjunction used to subordinate clauses which contain no other interrogative word and which would be, as principal clauses, questions of the "yes/no" type. Students who do not actively use <u>whether</u> in English tend to confuse it with the conjunction <u>se</u> used in "conditional sentences" (see ¶3.4.3 and note 59.)

51. Use of the future tense in the subordinate core is not infrequent after a future principal core but not obligatory.

Actuality	Anticipation

Io faccio <u>perchè me lo chiedono</u>   Io faccio <u>perchè non mi credano pazzo</u>

siamo partiti <u>prima che sei arrivato</u>   vattene <u>prima che ti vedano</u>

tutto andò bene <u>finchè egli rimase qui</u>   aspettiamo <u>finchè non[52] venga il fat-torino</u>

3.4.4. AS MODIFIERS IN SUBSTANTIVE OR PRONOUN PHRASES

These are <u>che</u> clauses and relative clauses—that is, clauses in which any slot within the subject or the predicate is occupied by a relative word.

<u>che</u> clauses:

la speranza <u>che il lavoro andrà bene</u>

(siamo) sicuri <u>che tutto è a posto</u>

When the center substantive inherently expresses uncertainty or emotion—<u>paura</u>, <u>-con-tent-</u>, <u>liet-</u>—the <u>che</u> core is automatically subjunctive:

(ho) paura <u>che lui sia cattivo</u>

(siamo) molto contenti <u>che siate venuti</u>

(non sono) sicura che Luigi possa farlo[53]

Relative clauses:

(non conosco) quel ragazzo
$\begin{cases} \text{che ci ha salutati} \\ \text{che tu hai salutato} \\ \text{di cui mi hai parlato} \\ \text{a cui hai dato il libro} \\ \text{il cui padre è professore} \end{cases}$

(ecco) la casa
$\begin{cases} \text{in cui abita Maria} \\ \text{nella quale abita Maria} \\ \text{dove abita Maria} \end{cases}$

Such sets of relative clauses as:

---

52. The use of a "pleonastic" <u>non</u>—for which of course there is no English counterpart—gives this conjunction the meaning <u>until</u> as against <u>as long as</u>. Even in anticipations, <u>finchè</u> without <u>non</u> does not bring on the subjunctive: <u>rimarrò qui finchè starai lavorando</u>.

53. It is of course the combination of the negative core and this particular center of the subjective complement that conveys the uncertainty.

quel signore che è stato così bravo	il bambino che ho visto
quella signora che è stata così brava	la bambina che ho vista
quei signori che sono stati così bravi	i bambini che ho visti
quelle signore che sono state così brave	le bambine che ho viste

show how G/N concord operates when che fills either the subject or the accusative complement slot. The linkage of either the perfective-core participle (stat-, vist-) or the subjective complement (brav-) is with che, which covertly carries the G/N reflected upon it by the substantival center which the clause modifies.[54]

Use of the subjunctive in relative clauses is never automatic, but it may be selected. It occurs chiefly when the embedding substantive (or pronoun) phrase is an accusative complement, and it indicates that a given qualification is anticipated, desired, or sought for to the exclusion of others:

(preferiamo impiegare) delle segretarie che sappiano l'inglese

(cerchiamo) un ragazzo che lavori con più entusiasmo

(offriamogli) tutto quello[55] che desideri avere

3.4.5. SEQUENCE OF TENSES

In discussing this principle, let us refer once more to the tense-mood box on p. 69. Generally speaking, a subordinate core in Italian may occur in any tense if the main core is "above the line." But if the principal core is "below the line," the subordinate core must also be below the line. Certain parallels with English tense sequence are of considerable help here:

I know that he	goes	went
	will go	would go
I knew that he	goes	went
	will go	would go

---

54. When che or cui is replaced by the relative substantive quale modified by the definite article, this determiner overtly marks the concord.

55. The demonstrative pronoun quell- modified by a relative clause gives no special trouble when it cross-refers to an elsewhere-located substantive: quelle che vedete (say, case) = the ones (that) you see. But when the m/s quello (or ciò) does not cross-refer, it causes difficulty in that its English counterpart that which is usually replaced by what. The student fails to distinguish this what from the interrogative what (= che), and so tends to say *che vedete for quello che vedete and likewise *tutto che vedete for tutto quello che vedete, a false analogy reinforced by English all (that) you see.

Unfortunately for the student, however, the marginal use of the English subjunctive does not involve tense sequence, because the verb has no present-past contrast in the subjunctive: so I insist that he go, and also I insisted that he go. This can dim the student's perception of the tense-sequence principle in Italian subjunctive clauses. The fact that to verbals are tenseless anyway (I want him to go, I wanted him to go) may dim it further. He needs to be drilled extensively in the transforming of principal and subordinate cores from above-the-line sequences to below-the-line sequences:

voglio che tu ci vada—volevo che tu ci andassi[56]

All the examples of subordinate clauses given in ¶3.4.1-4 were deliberately restricted to above-the-line sequences for simplicity. We may now profitably illustrate tense sequence in Italian with a selected few of our above examples, adding relevant comments in the footnotes:

Above the line	Below the line
risulta che ha ragione Lei	è risultato[57] che aveva ragione Lei
è vero che siamo felici	era vero che eravamo[58] felici
bisogna che me lo dica, però	bisognava che me lo dicessi, però
mi pare che ci sia stato uno sbaglio	mi pareva che ci fosse stato uno sbaglio
non è chiaro che ci sia altro da fare	non era chiaro che ci fosse altro da fare
sarà necessario che gli scriva	sarebbe necessario che gli scrivessi
sappiamo che lui non può venire	sapevamo che lui non poteva venire
vuoi che rimanga con te	volevi che rimanessi con te

56. Another useful drill supplies the student with clauses to be subordinated in various environments calling for the subjunctive:
Giuseppe viene oggi — non credo che Giuseppe venga oggi
ci aspetteranno qui — può darsi che ci aspettino qui
chi era quell'uomo — non sapevo chi fosse quell'uomo
ha studiato (= studiò) di più — ho insistito che studiasse di più
tutti andrebbero via = speravo che tutti andassero via
This reinforces the realization that any tense above the line gets replaced by the present subjunctive, while any tense below the line gets replaced by the past subjunctive. Drills should also include the imperative as replaceable by the present subjunctive:
imparate questo — voglio che impariate questo
57. This perfective core is a replacement for the preterit risultò, and therefore belongs below the line. But perfective presents in their own right are above the line; thus we may get also: è risultato che ha ragione Lei.
58. Subordinate present tenses typically become imperfects when shifted below the line.

credo che sia troppo tardi	credevo che fosse troppo tardi
gli ho domandato se tutto va bene	gli ho domandato (= domandai) se tutto andava bene
finiranno il loro compito se potranno	finirebbero il loro compito se potessero[59]
te lo darò quando ritornerò da Torino	te lo darei quando ritornassi da Torino
lo scriverà volentieri purchè glielo paghino	lo scriverebbe volentieri purchè glielo pagassero
lo faccio perchè me lo chiedono	l'ho fatto perchè me l'hanno chiesto
lo faccio perchè non mi credano pazzo	l'ho fatto perchè non mi credessero pazzo
(ho) paura che lui sia cattivo	(avevo) paura che lui fosse cattivo
(non conosco) quel ragazzo che ci ha salutati	(non conoscevo) quel ragazzo che ci aveva salutati

3.5. EXPRESSIONS OF COMPARISON AND OF NEGATION

Every language has some types of expression, each of which displays its characteristic features of internal structure and each of which may occur embedded in larger constructions of more than one sort. Two such types of expression which have high frequency in both Italian and English are expressions of comparison and expressions of negation. Each of these cross-cutting types could be given special attention in connection with each larger construction in which it participates—for example, comparison could be treated successively under substantive phrases, adjectival modifiers, adverb phrases, and so on—but to do this would be to obscure, from the student's point of view, its common features. We have therefore reserved the discussion of comparison and negation for a final separate section, thus directing attention to the essential problems of each.

3.5.1. COMPARISON

Expressions of comparison are of two sorts: comparisons of inequality, and comparisons of equality. The first is of considerably higher frequency, in both languages, than the second.

---

59. Compare also <u>avrebbero finito il loro compito se avessero potuto</u>. SE-clauses are most characteristically attributive to future or conditional cores in so-called "conditional sentences." Above the line, the subjunctive never occurs; but below the line, in the expression of a doubtful or negated ("contrary-to-fact") hypothesis, the subjunctive is, on the other hand, obligatory. Here it is worth while to draw a parallel with the contrast available with <u>be</u> alone in English: <u>if I was able</u> versus <u>if I were able</u> [but I am not]. Clauses subordinated by <u>come se</u>, by their very nature, occur only in the past subjunctive: <u>rispondi come se fossi sicuro</u>.

3.5.1.1. COMPARISONS OF INEQUALITY

These expressions always contain one of the quantifiers p<u>iù</u> or <u>meno</u>.[60] The difference between comparative and superlative degrees is not made formally in Italian, as it is in English by the contrast between <u>more</u> and <u>most</u>, <u>less</u> and <u>least</u>, <u>-er</u> and <u>-est</u>. This is not a source of interference for the learner, however, since he easily enough equates both degrees with p<u>iù</u> (or <u>meno</u>), and since the superlative in both languages is typically signaled in any instance by the presence of the definite article:[61]

> a better way = un miglior modo more important cities = città più importanti
> the best way = il miglior modo the most important cities = le città più importanti

Expressions of comparative degree always balance one "item" against another, implicitly or explicitly. The second item is often merely implicit—that is, understood from context and therefore not expressed: <u>Giovanni è piu alto</u> = <u>John is taller</u>. But when the second item is expressed, there is only one subordinator word to introduce it in English: <u>than</u>. In Italian, there are two: <u>di</u> and <u>che</u>. This, then, presents a problem to the learner. It is perhaps best approached by taking <u>di</u> as the norm, as used except in a few specific situations. Instances of the normal <u>di</u> may be illustrated plentifully:

> Giovanni è più alto <u>di Carlo</u>
> io studio più <u>di mio fratello</u>
> noi abbiamo più tempo di <u>voi</u>
> ci starò per più <u>di un anno</u>
> mi occorre una borsa più grande <u>di questa</u>
> ce n'erano meno <u>di cento</u>
> Caterina scrive con più immaginazione <u>delle altre ragazze</u>
> Paolo parla inglese molto meglio <u>di me</u>

It can then be stated that there are three conditions under which the second item is introduced by <u>che</u> instead of by <u>di</u>. The second item is balanced against the very word modified by p<u>iù</u> (or <u>meno</u>):

---

60. The Type II substantives <u>migliore-</u>, <u>peggiore-</u>, <u>maggiore-</u> and <u>minore-</u>, as well as the adverbs <u>meglio</u> and <u>peggio</u>, may be classed as derived stems which contain an allomorph of p<u>iù</u>, since they participate in comparisons of the same kind as are built by p<u>iù</u> + substantive or p<u>iù</u> + adverb. They thus correspond morphologically to English forms carrying the comparative/superlative suffixes <u>-er</u> and <u>-est</u>.

61. The distinction between <u>the older one</u> and <u>the oldest one</u> is simply not made in Italian: both are <u>il più vecchio</u>.

abbiamo più bicchieri che piatti (cf. . . . più bicchieri di voi)

Giovanni è un ragazzo più stupido che mal educato

Both items are functioning as attributive complements in a verb phrase:

sarebbe meglio cominciare adesso che domani

quell'espressione si usa più nel nord che altrove

fa più freddo a Londra che a Roma

The second item is a verbal:

sarebbe meglio farlo adesso che lasciarlo per domani

l'inglese è meno difficile che io non credessi[62]

3.5.1.2. COMPARISONS OF EQUALITY

These expressions always contain either the quantifier tant- or, in limited environments, the adverb così where English uses the word as. In them also, as in comparisons of inequality, one item is balanced against another, implicitly or explicitly. The second item, when explicit, is introduced by quant- in expressions containing tant-, and by come (like the English second as) in those containing così. Expressions with tant- are commoner:

noi (non) abbiamo tanti soldi quanto voi

Giovanna è una ragazza tanto brava quanto Carla

io (non) studio tanto quanto mio fratello

(non) si mangia tanto bene qui quanto a Parigi

(non) abbiamo tanti bicchieri quanti piatti

We observe that tant- shows G/N concord with a substantive center, but not with an adjectival modifier. Quant- shows G/N concord only when it introduces a substantive balanced against the very word modified by tant-, as in the last example.

When tant- is a constituent of an adjectival modifier or of an adverbial, its place may be taken by così, with the second item introduced by come. Students are likely to prefer this alternative where it is available, since it so nearly matches English as (or so) . . . as. We repeat those of the above examples in which così . . . come can be substituted:

Giovanna è una ragazza così brava come Carla

(non) si mangia così bene qui come a Parigi

---

62. When the core is finite, the pleonastic non is customary.

3.5.2. NEGATION

In addition to the negative particle non, Italian has a set of negative words belonging to some of the parts of speech: the pronoun nulla, the quantifiers niente and nessun-, the adverbs mai and mica, the co-ordinator nè, the universals neanche ~ neppure and nemmeno. In a verb phrase, any one of these negative words may occur before the core, and in this position they are incompatible with the particle non. On the other hand, all may also follow the core, in which instance the core must contain non. Examples of each in both positions:

Pre-Core	Post-Core
nulla è dovuto ai portabagagli	non lasciate nulla sulle sedie
niente di tutto quello mi interessa	non mi interessa niente di tutto quello
nessuno ti crederà	non ti crederà nessuno
mai sono sceso laggiù	non sono mai sceso laggiù
mica potrei accettarlo	non potrei mica[63] accettarlo
nè l'uno nè l'altro mi piace	non mi piace nè l'uno nè l'altro
neanche (or neppure) Pietro lo sa	non lo sa neanche (or neppure) Pietro
nemmeno uno si è fermato	non si è fermato nemmeno uno

Negative words may both precede and follow a single core (nessuno l'ha mai fatto), and more than one may follow:

quell'uomo non da mai niente a nessuno

One English equivalent of the last example is of course:

that man doesn't ever give anything to anybody

English has negative counterparts to the words ever, anything, anybody: never, nothing, nobody. But standard English tolerates a maximum of one negative word, including the particle not, in any one verb phrase.[64] Thus English is equipped with a set of negative/non-negative pairs, which match the Italian negatives as follows:

---

63. Mai and mica belong to a small class of adverbs which typically stand immediately after the auxiliary in a complex core. Others in Italian are già, sempre. The class is larger in English, and includes not only (n)ever, already, always, but also usually, sometimes, frequently.
64. It is possible to say also he never gives anything to anybody, or he gives nothing to anybody ever, or to nobody does he ever give anything; but standard English simply does not permit two negative words to co-occur.

Italian	English	
	negative	non-negative
nulla ~ niente	nothing	anything
nessun-	no ~ none	any
	nobody ~ no one	anybody ~ anyone
mai	never	ever
(nè . . .) nè	(neither . . .) nor	(either . . .) or
neanche ~ neppure	neither	either

Education has trained countless English speakers who grew up using the "double negative" to shun it at all cost, and in the schoolroom even those who never used it have been made conscious of its particular inacceptability. As a consequence, many bring to the study of a foreign language a deep-seated tendency to avoid multiple negation. In endeavoring to do so in Italian, they seize upon the nearest non-negative equivalent available for, say, anything, and this turns out to be qualcosa, which basically means something. The close lexical association of the some- series with the any- series in English questions (do you see something : do you see anything) makes it seem only fair, at some point, to gloss anything as qualcosa as well as niente (and qualsiasi cosa!); yet this is how the trap is sprung. Corrective drill is necessary chiefly in the use of nulla ~ niente and nessun-, where alone the some-/any- confusion interferes. With the equivalents for (n)ever, (n)either, (n)or there is less margin for error; and it helps that anche ~ pure has a matching opposite in also ~ too. Transposition drills like:

nessuno viene (= no one is coming) → non viene nessuno

are perhaps a good starting point, as establishing the framework for subsequent practice with the patterns non _____ nessun-, non _____ niente, and so on, followed by non voglio _____, non prendo _____, and so on.

APPENDIX

In the following chart of the common irregular verbs of Italian, entries are made only in the slots where the alternant is unpredictable according to the patterns set forth in ¶ 2.1.1.4. Purposely omitted are all optional forms of lower general frequency than the expected forms or the entered irregular forms: for <u>deve-</u> the present <u>debbo(no)</u> <u>debba(no)</u> as optional alternants of the more usual <u>devo(no)</u> <u>deva(no)</u> along with <u>devi deve</u>. Each verb entered has a different total pattern of irregularity. Wherever more than one verb exhibits the same over-all pattern, a single sample is entered and a note below indicates what other verbs share the pattern. A series of notes follow the chart, with cross-references to the entries.

The numbers identify the forms as follows:

1 = 1st singular	4 = 1st plural
2 = 2nd singular	5 = 2nd plural
3 = 3rd singular	6 = 3rd plural

The column headed "Present" includes present subjunctive forms, identified by "S."

An arrow pointing to the corresponding preterit stem indicates that the participle is formed on that same stem with the addition of the alternant ending <u>-o</u> (e.g., <u>pars-o</u>).

A hyphen at the beginning of a stem indicates that this stem occurs only with prefixes: <u>-cede-</u> (ε), for example, occurs in <u>concede-</u> (ε), <u>procede-</u> (ε), and so on. Since the pattern of the stem is the same regardless of the prefix, the hyphen is useful as a cover symbol to avoid a separate entry for each stem. Similarly, any stem which occurs both with and without prefixes is entered only under the bare stem; thus <u>pone-</u> (o), for example, subsumes all its derivatives by prefixation: <u>compone-</u> (o), <u>impone-</u> (o), <u>espone-</u> (o), and so on, which are identical in pattern to <u>pone-</u> itself.

Basic Stem	Present	Preterit 1,3,6	Participle	Future	Other
		a-stems			
anda-	2,3,6 vá- 1,S1,2,3,6vád-			andr-	
dá		diede-			Pret.2,4,5 ⎫ dé- Past Sbj. ⎭
stá-		stette-			Pret.2,4,5 ⎫ sté- Past Sbj. ⎭
		e-stems			
ave-	1,2,3,6 há- S ábbi-	ebbe-		avr-	Imper.S. abbi- Imper.P.abbiate
cade-		cadde-		cadr-	
dole- (uɔ)		dolse-		dorr-	
dove-	1,2,3,6 ⎫ dev- S1,2,3,6⎭ S4,5 dobb-			dovr-	
pare-		parve-	←	parr-	
piace-[a]	1,6,S piacci-	piacque-			
pote- (uɔ)	1,6,S poss- 2 puọi 3 può			potr-	
rimane-		rimase-	rimasto	rimarr-	
sape-	1,2,3,6 sá- S sáppi-	séppe-		sapr-	
sole- (uɔ)	1,6,S sogli-		sólito		
tene- (iɛ)		ténne-		terr-	
vale-		válse-	←	varr-	
vede- (e)		vide-	visto	vedr-	
vole- (uɔ)	1,6,S vogli- 2 vuoi	volle-		vorr-	
		e-stems with strong infinitive			
beve- (e)		bevve-		Inf. bere	
-cede-(ɛ)		-cesse-	←		
chiede-		chiese-	chiesto		
chiude-[b]		chiuse-	←		
coce- (uɔ)	1,6 cuócci- S Sg.,6	cosse-	cotto		
coglie-(ɔ)[c]		colse-	colto		
conosce-(o)		conobbe-			
corre- (o)		corse-	←		
cresce-(e)		crebbe-			

Basic Stem	Present	Preterit 1,3,6	Participle	Future	Other
e-stems with strong infinitive (cont.)					
dice-	5 dite	disse-	detto	dir-	Imper.S. di / Inf.　dire
-duce-		dusse-	-dotto	-durr-	Inf. -durre
esse- (ε)	S sá- / 1,6 sono / 2 sei / 3 é / 5 siete	1,3 fú- / 6 fúrono	stato	sar-	Imperf. era- / Pret.4 fummo / Pret.2,5 }fo- / Past S } / Imper. síi, siáte
face-	S fácci-	fece-	fatto	far-	Inf. fare
fonde- (o)		fuse-	←		
-fulge-[d]		-fulse-	-fulto		
legge- (ε)[e]		lesse-	letto		
nasce-		nacque-	nato		
neglige-		neglesse-	negletto		
noce- (uɔ)	1,6,S nócci-	nocque-			
pinge-[d]		pinse-	pinto		
piove-		piovve-			
pone- (o)		pose-	posto	porr-	Inf. porre
prende- (ε)[f]		prese-	←		
-prime-		-presse-	←		
risponde-(o)		rispose-	risposto		
rompe- (o)		ruppe-	rotto		
scinde-		scisse-	←		
scrive-		scrisse-	scritto		
-siste-			-sistito		
-solve-(ɔ)[c]		solse-	-soluto		
sorge- (o)[d]		sorse-	sorto		
spegne-(e)		spense-	spento		
-sume-		-sunse-	-sunto		
-tingue-		-tinse-	-tinto		
torce-(ɔ)		torse-	torto		
trae-	1,6 S Sg.,6 }tragg-	trasse-	tratto	trarr-	Inf. trarre
vince-		vinse-	vinto		
vive-		visse-	vissuto	vivr-	
i-stems					
apri-[g]		aperse-	aperto		
cuci-	1,6 S Sg.,6 }cúci-				

Basic Stem	Present	Preterit 1,3,6	Participle	Future	Other
		i-stems (cont.)			
mori- (uɔ)			morto		
-pari-		-parse-	←		
udi-	1,2,3,6 } od- S Sg.,6				
usci-	1,2,3,6 } esc- S Sg.,6				
veni- (iɛ)		venne-	venuto	verr-	

Notes to Chart

[a] Identical in pattern are giace- and tace-.

[b] Unless entered as otherwise irregular, all e stems in which the stem vowel is preceded by -d- or -rd- (but not -nd-; see Note f) have this pattern; thus also -clude-, rade-, arde-, etc. By exception, perde- (ɛ) has regular forms much in use, notably the participle perduto.

[c] So also sceglie- (e), scioglie- (ɔ), and toglie- (ɔ).

[d] Unless entered as otherwise irregular, all e stems in which the stem vowel is preceded by -ng-, -rg-, -lg- have this pattern; so also finge-, piange-, tinge-, accorge- (ɔ), indulge-, etc.

[e] All e stems in -gg- have this pattern; so also frigge-, strugge-, etc.

[f] Unless entered as otherwise irregular, all e stems in -nd- (cf. Note b) have this pattern with loss of -n-; thus also accende- (ɛ), rende- (ɛ), tunde-, etc. By exception, however, the stem vende- (e) is wholly regular.

[g] So also copri-, offri-, and soffri-, with -ɛ- inserted before the -r-.

INDEX